3/95

This book is to be returned on or before
the last date stamped below.

5 JUN 1996

22 JUL 1999

CW01102930

LIBREX

RINGWOOD SCHOOL
GRANT MAINTAINED COMPREHENSIVE
LIBRARY

RINGWOOD SCHOOL
GRANT MAINTAINED COMPREHENSIVE
LIBRARY

CollinsEducational
An imprint of HarperCollinsPublishers

ISBN 0 00 323037 6

© 1993 CollinsEducational

Roger Samways asserts the moral right to be identified as the author of this work.

All rights reserved. No part of this publication may be reproduced, stored in a retrieval system, or transmitted in any form or by any other means, electronic, mechanical, photocopying, recording, or otherwise, without the prior permission of the Copyright owner.

First published by CollinsEducational, *an imprint of* HarperCollins *Publishers* 77–85 Fulham Palace Road, London W6 8JB.

Cover and text designed by Christie Archer

Cover illustration by Neil Dishington

Edited by Philippa Sawyer

Production by James Graves

Typeset by Wyvern Typesetting Limited

Printed by Scotprint Ltd, Musselburgh

Acknowledgements

Special thanks are due to Nora Barnes of Puddletown for her help during the planning stage of this book. The authors and publishers would also like to thank the following for permission to reproduce illustrations:

Bridgeman Art Library: p. 101; Dorset County Museum: pp. 9, 42, 61; Dorset Centre for Educational Technology (photographs by Ian Condon): pp. 20, 32, 38, 44, 50, 65, 92, 99; J. Stevens Cox: p. 104 (both); The Serpent Press: p. 137.

Illustrations on pp. 15 and 139 by Robert Geary.

CONTENTS

THOMAS HARDY (1840–1928)   v

FAR FROM THE MADDING CROWD
Bathsheba Everdene: the men in her life   2

Poems 1
The Vampirine Fair   40
At a Watering-Place   42
The Dark-Eyed Gentleman   43

THE MAYOR OF CASTERBRIDGE
Michael Henchard: his rise and fall   46

Poems 2
Rose-Ann   71
The Wedding Morning   71
Julie-Jane   72

TESS OF THE D'URBERVILLES
Tess Durbeyfield: beloved and betrayed   74

Poems 3
The Ruined Maid   100
Tess's Lament   102

SHORT STORIES: A FEW CRUSTED CHARACTERS
Introduction   106
Tony Kytes, the Arch-Deceiver   109
The History of the Hardcomes   117
The Superstitious Man's Story   125
Andrey Satchel and the Parson and Clerk   128
Absent-Mindedness in a Parish Choir   138
Incident in the Life of Mr. George Crookhill   149

Thomas Hardy (1840–1928)

Thomas Hardy, novelist, poet and short story writer, was born in June 1840 in rural Dorset and grew up during the early years of Queen Victoria's reign. His father was a stone-mason, as well as being a leading musician in the local church and community life, at a time when 'choirs', or bands of instrumentalists, provided live music for church services and village dances.

It seemed quite natural, therefore, for Thomas, on leaving school in 1856, to learn his trade with a local architect in Dorchester and to begin to specialise in church architecture. At the same time he lived at home, amongst family and friends, eventually moving to London for five years to extend his experience and skills as an architect. It was during this period that he began to write poetry.

He returned to Dorchester in 1867 to work as assistant to John Hicks with whose firm he had served his apprenticeship. During this time he began writing his first novel.

It was on a working trip to Cornwall in 1870, to prepare plans for the re-building of St. Juliot church, near Boscastle, that Hardy met Emma Gifford. Their relationship flourished and by 1874 they were married and had settled in London.

Meanwhile one of his early novels, *Far from the Madding Crowd*, had been such a success that Hardy was able to give up working as an architect and make his living as a writer.

Over the next twenty years he wrote and successfully published more than a dozen full length novels and many varied short stories. Almost all of his work reflected life in rural Wessex (see map on page vi). Having always written poetry, he continued to do so in the remaining years of his life, publishing most of his poetry between 1897 and his death in 1928.

His wife, Emma, had died in 1912 and Hardy had married again in 1914. Although he had become a popular figure in London's literary circles since the mid 1870s, Hardy eventually settled in his native Dorset in 1883, moving two years later into Max Gate, a house he designed and had built for himself and which can still be seen in the county town of Dorchester.

Some of Hardy's novels caused a sensation when they were first published, notably *Tess of the D'Urbervilles* (1891) and *Jude the Obscure* (1896). These, and others like them, such as *Far from the Madding Crowd*, *The Mayor of Casterbridge* and *The Woodlanders* told powerful stories of relationships between men and women – love, marriage, seduction, betrayal – which were often complicated by the tensions of class and social etiquette. There were some aspects of *Tess of the D'Urbervilles* and *Jude the Obscure* which clearly offended the public taste of the late nineteenth century: but critical voices were in the minority and Hardy's novels proved to be extremely popular in weekly family magazines and newspapers such as *The Cornhill*, *The Graphic* and the American *Harpers Bazaar Magazine*.

A hundred years on from Hardy's time, public taste is less easily offended by serialised stories, now most commonly in the form of television soap operas. It should not be too difficult, however, to imagine how readers in the late nineteenth century eagerly waited for the next edition of the magazine to find out how Hardy was going to develop the story of his heroes and heroines.

In the sections which follow you will find extracts from *Far from the Madding Crowd* as well as *The Mayor of Casterbridge* and *Tess of the D'Urbervilles*. The final section is made up of a collection of Hardy's short stories called *A Few Crusted Characters*. A number of poems have been included to reflect the overall theme of the anthology.

> Ache deep; but make no moans:
> Smile out; but stilly suffer:
> The paths of love are rougher
> Than thoroughfares of stone.

(*from* The End of the Episode *in* Time's Laughing Stocks & Other Verses)

Map of Thomas Hardy's Wessex, with his fictional place-names. Hardy adopted the name 'Wessex' when he was writing Far from the Madding Crowd. In the preface he wrote: 'I first ventured to adopt the word Wessex from the pages of early English history. The series of novels I projected . . . seemed to require a territorial definition'.

The same geographical area today with the actual place names.

Far from the Madding Crowd

Bathsheba Everdene: the men in her life

Henry James, himself a novelist, in a review of **Far from the Madding Crowd** *in December 1874, gives us a neat summary of the plot:*

'Mr Hardy describes nature with a great deal of felicity, and is evidently much at home among rural phenomena. The most genuine thing in his book, to our sense, is a certain aroma of the meadows and lanes — a natural relish for harvestings and sheep-washings. He has laid his scene in an agricultural county, and his characters are children of the soil — unsophisticated country folk.

Bathsheba Everdene is a country heiress, left alone in the world, in possession of a substantial farm. Gabriel Oak is her shepherd, Farmer Boldwood is her neighbour, and Sergeant Troy is a loose young soldier who comes a-courting her. They are all in love with her, and the young lady is a flirt and encourages them all. Finally she marries the sergeant, who has just seduced her maid-servant. The maid-servant dies in the work house, the sergeant repents, leaves his wife and is given up for drowned. But he re-appears and is shot by Boldwood who delivers himself up to justice. Bathsheba then marries Gabriel Oak, who has loved and waited in silence, and is, in our opinion, much too good for her.'

The three men whose paths cross as they encounter the beautiful Bathsheba Everdene, were concisely described by an anonymous writer reviewing the novel when it was first published in serial form by **The Cornhill Magazine** *in 1874:*

'The man of single eye, who waits and works patiently, scarcely hoping even for recognition, but ready to help the woman he loves, literally through fire and water.' (Gabriel Oak)

'The profligate soldier, who comes, sees, and, for a time, conquers.' (Sergeant Frank Troy)

'The reserved, middle-aged farmer, falling in love for the first time at forty, and then driven almost, if not quite, to insanity by disappointment.' (Farmer Boldwood)

Far from the Madding Crowd

Gabriel Oak has come to work as a shepherd for Bathsheba Everdene and is looking for lodgings. The farm bailiff suggests that he should go to Warren's Malthouse, where the locals always congregate to eat and drink.

Warren's Malthouse was enclosed by an old wall inwrapped with ivy, and though not much of the exterior was visible at this hour, the character and purposes of the building were clearly enough shown by its outline upon the sky. From the walls an overhanging thatched roof sloped up to a point in the centre, upon which rose a small wooden lantern, fitted with louvre-boards on all the four sides, and from these openings a mist was dimly perceived to be escaping into the night air. There was no window in front; but a square hole in the door was glazed with a single pane, through which red, comfortable rays now stretched out upon the ivied wall in front. Voices were to be heard inside.

Oak's hand skimmed the surface of the door till he found a leathern strap, which he pulled. This lifted a wooden latch, and the door swung open.

The room inside was lighted only by the ruddy glow from the kiln mouth, which shone over the floor with the streaming horizontality of the setting sun, and threw upwards the shadows of all facial irregularities in those assembled around. The stone-flag floor was worn into a path from the doorway to the kiln, and into undulations everywhere. A curved settle of unplaned oak stretched along one side, and in a remote corner was a small bed and bedstead, the owner and frequent occupier of which was the maltster.

This aged man was now sitting opposite the fire, his frosty white hair and beard overgrowing his gnarled figure like the grey moss and lichen upon a leafless apple-tree. He wore breeches and the laced-up shoes called ankle-jacks; he kept his eyes fixed upon the fire.

Gabriel's nose was greeted by an atmosphere laden with the sweet smell of new malt. The conversation (which seemed to have been concerning the origin of the fire) immediately ceased, and every one ocularly criticized him to the degree expressed by contracting the flesh of their foreheads and looking at him with narrowed eyelids, as if he had been a light too strong for their sight. Several exclaimed meditatively, after this operation had been completed: –

'Oh, 'tis the new shepherd, 'a b'lieve.'

'We thought we heard a hand pawing about the door for the bobbin,* but weren't sure 'twere not a dead leaf blowed across,' said another.

---

* bobbin: rounded piece of wood attached to a latch-string

'Come in, shepherd; sure ye be welcome, though we don't know yer name.'

'Gabriel Oak, that's my name, neighbours.'

The ancient maltster sitting in the midst turned at this – his turning being as the turning of a rusty crane.

'That's never Gable Oak's grandson over at Norcombe – never!' he said, as a formula expressive of surprise, which nobody was supposed to take literally.

'My father and my grandfather were old men of the name of Gabriel,' said the shepherd placidly.

'Thought I knowed the man's face as I seed him on the rick! – thought I did! And where be ye trading o't to now, shepherd?'

'I'm thinking of biding here,' said Mr. Oak.

'Knowed yer grandfather for years and years!' continued the maltster, the words coming forth of their own accord as if the momentum previously imparted had been sufficient.

'Ah – and did you!'

'Knowed yer grandmother.'

'And her too!'

'Likewise knowed yer father when he was a child. Why, my boy Jacob there and your father were sworn brothers – that they were sure – weren't ye Jacob?'

'Ay, sure,' said his son, a young man about sixty-five, with a semi-bald head and one tooth in the left centre of his upper jaw, which made much of itself by standing prominent, like a milestone in a bank. 'But 'twas Joe had most to do with him. However, my son William must have knowed the very man afore us – didn't ye, Billy, afore ye left Norcombe?'

'No, 'twas Andrew,' said Jacob's son Billy, a child of forty, or thereabouts, who manifested the peculiarity of possessing a cheerful soul in a gloomy body, and whose whiskers were assuming a chinchilla shade here and there.

'I can mind Andrew,' said Oak, 'as being a man in the place when I was quite a child.'

'Ay – the other day I and my youngest daughter, Liddy, were over at my grandson's christening,' continued Billy. 'We were talking about this very family, and 'twas only last Purification Day* in this very world, when the use-money* is gied away to the second-best poor folk, you know, shepherd, and I can mind the day because they all had to traypse up to the vestry – yes, this very man's family.'

'Come, shepherd, and drink. 'Tis gape and swaller with us – a drap of sommit, but not of much account,' said the maltster, removing from the

---

* Purification Day: 2nd February. Also known as Candlemas Day.

* use-money: (dialect) interest on money i.e. on some charitable endowment

fire his eyes, which were vermilion-red and bleared by gazing into it for so many years. 'Take up the God-forgive-me, Jacob. See if 'tis warm, Jacob.'

Jacob stooped to the God-forgive-me, which was a two-handled tall mug standing in the ashes, cracked and charred with heat: it was rather furred with extraneous matter about the outside, especially in the crevices of the handles, the innermost curves of which may not have seen daylight for several years by reason of this encrustation thereon – formed of ashes accidentally wetted with cider and baked hard; but to the mind of any sensible drinker the cup was no worse for that, being incontestably clean on the inside and about the rim. It may be observed that such a class of mug is called a God-forgive-me in Weatherbury and its vicinity for uncertain reasons; probably because its size makes any given toper feel ashamed of himself when he sees its bottom in drinking it empty.

Jacob, on receiving the order to see if the liquor was warm enough, placidly dipped his forefinger into it by way of thermometer, and having pronounced it nearly of the proper degree, raised the cup and very civilly attempted to dust some of the ashes from the bottom with the skirt of his smock-frock, because Shepherd Oak was a stranger.

'A clane cup for the shepherd,' said the maltster commandingly.

'No – not at all,' said Gabriel, in a reproving tone of considerateness. 'I never fuss about dirt in its pure state, and when I know what sort it is.' Taking the mug he drank an inch or more from the depth of its contents, and duly passed it to the next man. 'I wouldn't think of giving such trouble to neighbours in washing up when there's so much work to be done in the world already,' continued Oak in a moister tone, after recovering from the stoppage of breath which is occasioned by pulls at large mugs.

'A right sensible man,' said Jacob.

'True, true; it can't be gainsaid!' observed a brisk young man – Mark Clark by name, a genial and pleasant gentleman, whom to meet anywhere in your travels was to know, to know was to drink with, and to drink with was, unfortunately, to pay for.

'And here's a mouthful of bread and bacon that mis'ess have sent, shepherd. The cider will go down better with a bit of victuals. Don't ye chaw quite close, shepherd, for I let the bacon fall in the road outside as I was bringing it along, and may be 'tis rather gritty. There, 'tis clane dirt; and we all know what that is, as you say, and you bain't a particular man we see, shepherd.'

'True, true – not at all,' said the friendly Oak.

'Don't let your teeth quite meet, and you won't feel the sandiness at all. Ah! 'tis wonderful what can be done by contrivance!'

'My own mind exactly, neighbour.'

'Ah, he's his grandfer's own grandson! – his grandfer were just such a nice unparticular man!' said the maltster.

'Drink, Henry Fray – drink,' magnanimously said Jan Coggan, a person who held notions of share and share alike where liquor was concerned, as the vessel showed signs of approaching him in its gradual revolution among them.

Having at this moment reached the end of a wistful gaze into midair, Henry did not refuse. He was a man of more than middle age, with eyebrows high up in his forehead, who laid it down that the law of the world was bad, with a long-suffering look through his listeners at the world alluded to, as it presented itself to his imagination. He always signed his name 'Henery' – strenuously insisting upon that spelling, and if any passing schoolmaster ventured to remark that the second 'e' was superfluous and old-fashioned, he received the reply that 'H-e-n-e-r-y' was the name he was christened and the name he would stick to – in the tone of one to whom orthographical differences were matters which had a great deal to do with personal character.

Mr. Jan Coggan, who had passed the cup to Henery, was a crimson man with a spacious countenance and private glimmer in his eye, whose name had appeared on the marriage register of Weatherbury and neighbouring parishes as best man and chief witness in countless unions of the previous twenty years; he also very frequently filled the post of head godfather in baptisms of the subtly-jovial kind.

'Come, Mark Clark – come. Ther's plenty more in the barrel,' said Jan.

'Ay – that I will; 'tis my only doctor,' replied Mr. Clark, who, twenty years younger than Jan Coggan, revolved in the same orbit. He secreted mirth on all occasions for special discharge at popular parties.

'Why, Joseph Poorgrass, ye han't had a drop!' said Mr. Coggan to a self-conscious man in the background, thrusting the cup towards him.

'Such a modest man as he is!' said Jacob Smallbury. 'Why, ye've hardly had strength of eye enough to look in our young mis'ess's face, so I hear, Joseph?'

All looked at Joseph Poorgrass with pitying reproach.

'No – I've hardly looked at her at all,' simpered Joseph, reducing his body smaller whilst talking, apparently from a meek sense of undue prominence. 'And when I seed her, 'twas nothing but blushes with me!'

'Poor feller,' said Mr. Clark.

''Tis a curious nature for a man,' said Jan Coggan.

'Yes,' continued Joseph Poorgrass – his shyness, which was so painful as a defect, filling him with a mild complacency now that it was regarded as an interesting study. ''Twere blush, blush, blush with me every minute of the time, when she was speaking to me.'

'I believe ye, Joseph Poorgrass, for we all know ye to be a very bashful man.'

''Tis a' awkward gift for a man, poor soul,' said the maltster. 'And ye have suffered from it a long time, we know.'

'Ay, ever since I was a boy. Yes – mother was concerned to her heart about it – yes. But 'twas all nought.'

'Did ye ever go into the world to try and stop it, Joseph Poorgrass?'

'Oh ay, tried all sorts o' company. They took me to Greenhill Fair, and into a great gay jerry-go-nimble show,* where there were women-folk riding round – standing upon horses, with hardly anything on but their smocks; but it didn't cure me a morsel. And then I was put errand-man at the Women's Skittle Alley at the back of the Tailor's Arms in Casterbridge. 'Twas a horrible sinful situation, and a very curious place for a good man. I had to stand and look ba'dy* people in the face from morning till night; but 'twas no use – I was just as bad as ever after all. Blushes hev been in the family for generations. There, 'tis a happy providence that I be no worse.'

'True,' said Jacob Smallbury, deepening his thoughts to a profounder view of the subject. ''Tis a thought to look at, that ye might have been worse; but even as you be, 'tis a very bad affliction for 'ee, Joseph. For ye see, shepherd, though 'tis very well for a woman, dang it all, 'tis awkward for a man like him, poor feller?'

''Tis – 'tis,' said Gabriel, recovering from a meditation. 'Yes, very awkward for the man.'

'Ay, and he's very timid, too,' observed Jan Coggan. 'Once he had been working late at Yalbury Bottom, and had had a drap of drink, and lost his way as he was coming home-along through Yalbury Wood, didn't ye, Master Poorgrass?'

'No, no, no; not that story!' expostulated the modest man, forcing a laugh to bury his concern.

' – And so 'a lost himself quite,' continued Mr. Coggan, with an impassive face, implying that a true narrative, like time and tide, must run its course and would respect no man. 'And as he was coming along in the middle of the night, much afeared, and not able to find his way out of the trees nohow, 'a cried out, "Man-a-lost! man-a-lost!" A owl in a tree happened to be crying "Whoo-whoo-whoo!" as owls do, you know, shepherd' (Gabriel nodded), 'and Joseph, all in a tremble, said, "Joseph Poorgrass, of Weatherbury, sir!"'

'No, no, now – that's too much!' said the timid man, becoming a man of brazen courage all of a sudden. 'I didn't say *sir*. I'll take my oath I didn't say "Joseph Poorgrass o' Weatherbury, sir." No, no; what's right

---

* jerry-go-nimble show: (dialect) circus
* ba'dy: (dialect) bawdy; lewd

is right, and I never said sir to the bird, knowing very well that no man of a gentleman's rank would be hollering there at that time o' night. "Joseph Poorgrass of Weatherbury," – that's every word I said, and I shouldn't ha' said that if't hadn't been for Keeper Day's metheglin.* ... There, 'twas a merciful thing it ended where it did.'

The question of which was right being tacitly waived by the company, Jan went on meditatively: –

'And he's the fearfullest man, bain't ye, Joseph? Ay, another time ye were lost by Lambing-Down Gate, weren't ye, Joseph?'

'I was,' replied Poorgrass, as if there were some conditions too serious even for modesty to remember itself under, this being one.

'Yes; that were the middle of the night, too. The gate would not open, try how he would, and knowing there was the Devil's hand in it, he kneeled down.'

'Ay,' said Joseph, acquiring confidence from the warmth of the fire, the cider, and a perception of the narrative capabilities of the experience alluded to. 'My heart died within me, that time; but I kneeled down and said the Lord's Prayer, and then the Belief right through, and then the Ten Commandments, in earnest prayer. But no, the gate wouldn't open; and then I went on with Dearly Beloved Brethren, and, thinks I, this makes four, and 'tis all I know out of book, and if this don't do it nothing will, and I'm a lost man. Well, when I got to Saying After Me, I rose from my knees and found the gate would open – yes, neighbours, the gate opened the same as ever.'

A meditation on the obvious inference was indulged in by all, and during its continuance each directed his vision into the ashpit, which glowed like a desert in the tropics under a vertical sun, shaping their eyes long and liny, partly because of the light, partly from the depth of the subject discussed.

Gabriel broke the silence. 'What sort of a place is this to live at, and what sort of a mis'ess is she to work under?' Gabriel's bosom thrilled gently as he thus slipped under the notice of the assembly the innermost subject of his heart.

'We d' know little of her – nothing. She only showed herself a few days ago. Her uncle was took bad, and the doctor was called with his world-wide skill; but he couldn't save the man. As I take it, she's going to keep on the farm.'

(Chapter 8)

---

* metheglin: a spiced form of mead

Max Gate, in Dorchester, the house Hardy designed and had built for himself and his wife, Emma, between 1883 and 1885.

Bathsheba soon shows her assembled workforce just 'what sort of mis'ess' she is to work under.

Half-an-hour later Bathsheba, in finished dress, and followed by Liddy, entered the upper end of the old hall to find that her men had all deposited themselves on a long form and a settle at the lower extremity. She sat down at a table and opened the time-book, pen in her hand, with a canvas money-bag beside her. From this she poured a small heap of coin. Liddy chose a position at her elbow and began to sew, sometimes pausing and looking round, or, with the air of a privileged person, taking up one of the half-sovereigns lying before her, and surveying it merely as a work of art, while strictly preventing her countenance from expressing any wish to possess it as money.

'Now, before I begin, men,' said Bathsheba, 'I have two matters to speak of. The first is that the bailiff is dismissed for thieving, and that I have formed a resolution to have no bailiff at all, but to manage everything with my own head and hands.'

The men breathed an audible breath of amazement.

'The next matter is, have you heard anything of Fanny?'

'Nothing, ma'am.'

'Have you done anything?'

'I met Farmer Boldwood,' said Jacob Smallbury, 'and I went with him and two of his men, and dragged Newmill Pond, but we found nothing.'

'And the new shepherd have been to Buck's Head, by Yalbury, thinking she had gone there, but nobody had seed her,' said Laban Tall.

'Hasn't William Smallbury been to Casterbridge?'

'Yes, ma'am, but he's not yet come home. He promised to be back by six.'

'It wants a quarter to six at present,' said Bathsheba, looking at her watch. 'I daresay he'll be in directly. Well, now then' – she looked into the book – 'Joseph Poorgrass, are you there?'

'Yes, sir – ma'am I mane,' said the person addressed. 'I be the personal name of Poorgrass.'

'And what are you?'

'Nothing in my own eye. In the eye of other people – well, I don't say it; though public thought will out.'

'What do you do on the farm?'

'I do do carting things all the year, and in seed time I shoots the rooks and sparrows, and helps at pig-killing, sir.'

'How much to you?'

'Please nine and ninepence and a good halfpenny where 'twas a bad one, sir – ma'am I mane.'

'Quite correct. Now here are ten shillings in addition as a small present, as I am a new comer.'

Bathsheba blushed slightly at the sense of being generous in public, and Henery Fray, who had drawn up towards her chair, lifted his eyebrows and fingers to express amazement on a small scale.

'How much do I owe you – that man in the corner – what's your name?' continued Bathsheba.

'Matthew Moon, ma'am,' said a singular framework of clothes with nothing of any consequence inside them, which advanced with the toes in no definite direction forwards, but turned in or out as they chanced to swing.

'Matthew Mark, did you say? – speak out – I shall not hurt you,' inquired the young farmer kindly.

'Matthew Moon, mem,' said Henery Fray, correctingly, from behind her chair, to which point he had edged himself.

'Matthew Moon,' murmured Bathsheba, turning her bright eyes to the book. 'Ten and twopence halfpenny is the sum put down to you, I see?'

'Yes, mis'ess,' said Matthew, as the rustle of wind among dead leaves.

'Here it is, and ten shillings. Now the next – Andrew Randle, you are a new man, I hear. How came you to leave your last farm?'

'P-p-p-p-p-pl-pl-pl-pl-l-l-l-l-ease, ma'am, p-p-p-p-pl-pl-pl-pl-please, ma'am-please'm-please'm –'

''A's a stammering man, mem,' said Henery Fray in an undertone, 'and they turned him away because the only time he ever did speak plain he said his soul was his own, and other iniquities, to the squire. 'A can cuss, mem, as well as you or I, but 'a can't speak a common speech to save his life.'

'Andrew Randle, here's yours – finish thanking me in a day or two. Temperance Miller – oh, here's another, Soberness – both women, I suppose?'

'Yes'm. Here we be, 'a b'lieve,' was echoed in shrill unison.

'What have you been doing?'

'Tending thrashing machine, and wimbling haybonds,* and saying "Hoosh!" to the cocks and hens when they go upon your seeds, and planting Early Flourballs and Thompson's Wonderfuls* with a dibble.'*

---

* wimbling haybonds: twisting hay into ropes with a wimble or gimlet
* Early Flourballs and Thompson's Wonderfuls: varieties of potato
* dibble: a pointed wooden tool for making seed-planting holes

'Yes – I see. Are they satisfactory women?' she inquired softly of Henery Fray.

'Oh mem – don't ask me! Yielding women – as scarlet a pair as ever was!' groaned Henery under his breath.

'Sit down.'

'Who, mem?'

'Sit down.'

Joseph Poorgrass, in the background, twitched, and his lips became dry with fear of some terrible consequences, as he saw Bathsheba summarily speaking, and Henery slinking off to a corner.

'Now the next. Laban Tall, you'll stay on working for me?'

'For you or anybody that pays me well, ma'am,' replied the young married man.

'True – the man must live!' said a woman in the back quarter, who had just entered with clicking pattens.*

'What woman is that?' Bathsheba asked.

'I be his lawful wife!' continued the voice with greater prominence of manner and tone. This lady called herself five-and-twenty, looked thirty, passed as thirty-five, and was forty. She was a woman who never, like some newly married, showed conjugal tenderness in public, perhaps she had none to show.

'Oh, you are,' said Bathsheba. 'Well, Laban, will you stay on?'

'Yes, he'll stay, ma'am!' said again the shrill tongue of Laban's lawful wife.

'Well, he can speak for himself, I suppose.'

'Oh Lord, not he, ma'am! A simple tool.* Well enough, but a poor gawkhammer* mortal,' the wife replied.

'Heh-heh-heh!' laughed the married man, with a hideous effort of appreciation, for he was as irrepressibly good-humoured under ghastly snubs as a parliamentary candidate on the hustings.

The names remaining were called in the same manner.

'Now I think I have done with you,' said Bathsheba, closing the book and shaking back a stray twine of hair. 'Has William Smallbury returned?'

'No, ma'am.'

'The new shepherd will want a man under him,' suggested Henery Fray, trying to make himself official again by a sideway approach towards her chair.

'Oh – he will. Who can he have?'

---

* pattens: wooden shoes
* tool: someone who is used by others
* gawkhammer: empty headed, scatter-brained

'Young Cain Ball is a very good lad,' Henery said, 'and Shepherd Oak don't mind his youth?' he added, turning with an apologetic smile to the shepherd, who had just appeared on the scene, and was now leaning against the doorpost with his arms folded.

'No, I don't mind that,' said Gabriel.

'How did Cain come by such a name?' asked Bathsheba.

'Oh you see, mem, his pore mother, not being a Scripture-read woman, made a mistake at his christening, thinking 'twas Abel killed Cain, and called en Cain, meaning Abel all the time. The parson put it right, but 'twas too late, for the name could never be got rid of in the parish. 'Tis very unfortunate for the boy.'

'It is rather unfortunate.'

'Yes. However, we soften it down as much as we can, and call him Cainy. Ah, pore widow-woman! she cried her heart out about it almost. She was brought up by a very heathen father and mother, who never sent her to church or school, and it shows how the sins of the parents are visited upon the children, mem.'

Mr. Fray here drew up his features to the mild degree of melancholy required when the persons involved in the given misfortune do not belong to your own family.

'Very well then, Cainy Ball to be under-shepherd. And you quite understand your duties? – you I mean, Gabriel Oak?'

'Quite well, I thank you, Miss Everdene,' said Shepherd Oak from the doorpost. 'If I don't, I'll inquire.' Gabriel was rather staggered by the remarkable coolness of her manner. Certainly nobody without previous information would have dreamt that Oak and the handsome woman before whom he stood had ever been other than strangers. But perhaps her air was the inevitable result of the social rise which had advanced her from a cottage to a large house and fields. The case is not unexampled in high places. When, in the writings of the later poets, Jove and his family are found to have moved from their cramped quarters on the peak of Olympus into the wide sky above it, their words show a proportionate increase of arrogance and reserve.

Footsteps were heard in the passage, combining in their character the qualities both of weight and measure, rather at the expense of velocity.

(All.) 'Here's Billy Smallbury come from Casterbridge.'

'And what's the news?' said Bathsheba, as William, after marching to the middle of the hall, took a handkerchief from his hat and wiped his forehead from its centre to its remoter boundaries.

'I should have been sooner, miss,' he said, 'if it hadn't been for the weather.' He then stamped with each foot severely, and on looking down his boots were perceived to be clogged with snow.

'Come at last, is it?' said Henery.

'Well, what about Fanny?' said Bathsheba.

'Well, ma'am, in round numbers, she's run away with the soldiers,' said William.

'No; not a steady girl like Fanny!'

'I'll tell ye all particulars. When I got to Casterbridge Barracks, they said, "The Eleventh Dragoon Guards be gone away, and new troops have come." The Eleventh left last week for Melchester and onwards. The Route* came from Government like a thief in the night, as is his nature to, and afore the Eleventh knew it almost, they were on the march. They passed near here.'

Gabriel had listened with interest. 'I saw them go,' he said.

'Yes,' continued William, 'they pranced down the street playing "The Girl I Left Behind Me", so 'tis said, in glorious notes of triumph. Every looker-on's inside shook with the blows of the great drum to his deepest vitals, and there was not a dry eye throughout the town among the public-house people and the nameless women!'

'But they're not gone to any war?'

'No, ma'am; but they be gone to take the places of them who may, which is very close connected. And so I said to myself, Fanny's young man was one of the regiment, and she's gone after him. There, ma'am, that's it in black and white.'

'Did you find out his name?'

'No; nobody knew it. I believe he was higher in rank than a private.'

Gabriel remained musing and said nothing, for he was in doubt.

'Well, we are not likely to know more to-night, at any rate,' said Bathsheba. 'But one of you had better run across to Farmer Boldwood's and tell him that much.'

She then rose; but before retiring, addressed a few words to them with a pretty dignity, to which her mourning dress added a soberness that was hardly to be found in the words themselves:

'Now mind, you have a mistress instead of a master. I don't yet know my powers or my talents in farming; but I shall do my best, and if you serve me well, so shall I serve you. Don't any unfair ones among you (if there are any such, but I hope not) suppose that because I'm a woman I don't understand the difference between bad goings-on and good.'

(All.) 'No'm!'

(Liddy.) 'Excellent well said.'

'I shall be up before you are awake; I shall be afield before you are up; and I shall have breakfasted before you are afield. In short, I shall astonish you all.'

(All.) 'Yes'm!'

'And so good-night.'

---

* Route: order to march

(All.) 'Good-night, ma'am.'

Then this small thesmothete* stepped from the table, and surged out of the hall, her black silk dress licking up a few straws and dragging them along with a scratching noise upon the floor. Liddy, elevating her feelings to the occasion from a sense of grandeur, floated off behind Bathsheba with a milder dignity not entirely free from travesty, and the door was closed.

(*Chapter 10*)

'Ten and twopence halfpenny is the sum put down to you, I see?' (see page 11)

---

* thesmothete : (Greek) law-giver

One of Bathsheba's servants, Fanny Robin, has disappeared. She is in pursuit of her 'young man', a soldier whose regiment has just moved out of Casterbridge barracks.

For dreariness nothing could surpass a prospect in the outskirts of a certain town and military station, many miles north of Weatherbury, at a later hour on this same snowy evening – if that may be called a prospect of which the chief constituent was darkness.

It was a night when sorrow may come to the brightest without causing any great sense of incongruity: when, with impressible persons, love becomes solicitousness, hope sinks to misgiving, and faith to hope: when the exercise of memory does not stir feelings of regret at opportunities for ambition that have been passed by, and anticipation does not prompt to enterprise.

The scene was a public path, bordered on the left hand by a river, behind which rose a high wall. On the right was a tract of land, partly meadow and partly moor, reaching, at its remote verge, to a wide undulating upland.

The changes of the seasons are less obtrusive on spots of this kind than amid woodland scenery. Still, to a close observer, they are just as perceptible; the difference is that their media of manifestation are less trite and familiar than such well-known ones as the bursting of the buds or the fall of the leaf. Many are not so stealthy and gradual as we may be apt to imagine in considering the general torpidity of a moor or waste. Winter, in coming to the country hereabout, advanced in well-marked stages, wherein might have been successively observed the retreat of the snakes, the transformation of the ferns, the filling of the pools, a rising of fogs, the embrowning by frost, the collapse of the fungi, and an obliteration by snow.

This climax of the series had been reached to-night on the aforesaid moor, and for the first time in the season its irregularities were forms without features; suggestive of anything, proclaiming nothing, and without more character than that of being the limit of something else – the lowest layer of a firmament of snow. From this chaotic skyful of crowding flakes the mead and moor momentarily received additional clothing, only to appear momentarily more naked thereby. The vast arch of cloud above was strangely low, and formed as it were the roof of a large dark cavern, gradually sinking in upon its floor; for the instinctive thought was that the snow lining the heavens and that encrusting the earth would soon unite into one mass without any intervening stratum of air at all.

We turn our attention to the left-hand characteristics; which were flatness in respect of the river, verticality in respect of the wall behind it, and darkness as to both. These features made up the mass. If anything could be darker than the sky, it was the wall, and if anything could be gloomier than the wall it was the river beneath. The indistinct summit of the façade was notched and prolonged by chimneys here and there, and upon its face were faintly signified the oblong shapes of windows, though only in the upper part. Below, down to the water's edge, the flat was unbroken by hole or projection.

An indescribable succession of dull blows, perplexing in their regularity, sent their sound with difficulty through the fluffy atmosphere. It was a neighbouring clock striking ten. The bell was in the open air, and being overlaid with several inches of muffling snow, had lost its voice for the time.

About this hour the snow abated: ten flakes fell where twenty had fallen, then one had the room of ten. Not long after a form moved by the brink of the river.

By its outline upon the colourless background a close observer might have seen that it was small. This was all that was positively discoverable, though it seemed human.

The shape went slowly along, but without much exertion, for the snow, though sudden, was not as yet more than two inches deep. At this time some words were spoken aloud: –

'One. Two. Three. Four. Five.'

Between each utterance the little shape advanced about half-a-dozen yards. It was evident now that the windows high in the wall were being counted. The word 'Five' represented the fifth window from the end of the wall.

Here the spot stopped, and dwindled smaller. The figure was stooping. Then a morsel of snow flew across the river towards the fifth window. It smacked against the wall at a point several yards from its mark. The throw was the idea of a man conjoined with the execution of a woman. No man who had ever seen a bird, rabbit, or squirrel in his childhood, could possibly have thrown with such utter imbecility as was shown here.

Another attempt, and another; till by degrees the wall must have become pimpled with the adhering lumps of snow. At last one fragment struck the fifth window.

The river would have been seen by day to be of that deep smooth sort which races middle and sides with the same gliding precision, any irregularities of speed being immediately corrected by a small whirlpool.

Nothing was heard in reply to the signal but the gurgle and cluck of one of these invisible wheels – together with a few small sounds which a sad man would have called moans, and a happy man laughter – caused by the flapping of the waters against trifling objects in other parts of the stream.

The window was struck again in the same manner.

Then a noise was heard, apparently produced by the opening of the window. This was followed by a voice from the same quarter:

'Who's there?'

The tones were masculine, and not those of surprise. The high wall being that of a barrack, and marriage being looked upon with disfavour in the army, assignations and communications had probably been made across the river before to-night.

'Is it Sergeant Troy?' said the blurred spot in the snow, tremulously.

This person was so much like a mere shade upon the earth, and the other speaker so much a part of the building, that one would have said the wall was holding a conversation with the snow.

'Yes,' came suspiciously from the shadow. 'What girl are you?'

'Oh, Frank – don't you know me?' said the spot. 'Your wife, Fanny Robin.'

'Fanny!' said the wall, in utter astonishment.

'Yes,' said the girl, with a half-suppressed gasp of emotion.

There was something in the woman's tone which is not that of the wife, and there was a manner in the man which is rarely a husband's. The dialogue went on:

'How did you come here?'

'I asked which was your window. Forgive me!'

'I did not expect you to-night. Indeed, I did not think you would come at all. It was a wonder you found me here. I am orderly to-morrow.'

'You said I was to come.'

'Well – I said that you might.'

'Yes, I mean that I might. You are glad to see me, Frank?'

'Oh yes – of course.'

'Can you – come to me?'

'My dear Fan, no! The bugle has sounded, the barrack gates are closed, and I have no leave. We are all of us as good as in the county gaol till to-morrow morning.'

'Then I shan't see you till then!' The words were in a faltering tone of disappointment.

'How did you get here from Weatherbury?'

'I walked – some part of the way – the rest by the carriers.'

'I am surprised.'

'Yes – so am I. And Frank, when will it be?'

'What?'
'That you promised.'
'I don't quite recollect.'
'Oh you do! Don't speak like that. It weighs me to the earth. It makes me say what ought to be said first by you.'
'Never mind – say it.'
'Oh, must I? – it is, when shall we be married, Frank?'
'Oh, I see. Well – you have to get proper clothes.'
'I have money. Will it be by banns or license?'
'Banns, I should think.'
'And we live in two parishes.'
'Do we? What then?'
'My lodgings are in St. Mary's, and this is not. So they will have to be published in both.'
'Is that the law?'
'Yes. Oh Frank – you think me forward, I am afraid! Don't, dear Frank – will you – for I love you so. And you said lots of times you would marry me, and – and I – I – I –'
'Don't cry, now! It is foolish. If I said so, of course I will.'
'And shall I put up the banns in my parish, and will you in yours?'
'Yes.'
'To-morrow?'
'Not to-morrow. We'll settle in a few days.'
'You have the permission of the officers?'
'No – not yet.'
'Oh – how is it? You said you almost had before you left Casterbridge.'
'The fact is, I forgot to ask. Your coming like this is so sudden and unexpected.'
'Yes – yes – it is. It was wrong of me to worry you. I'll go away now. Will you come and see me to-morrow, at Mrs. Twills's, in North Street? I don't like to come to the Barracks. There are bad women about, and they think me one.'
'Quite so. I'll come to you, my dear. Good-night.'
'Good-night, Frank – good-night!'
And the noise was again heard of a window closing. The little spot moved away. When she passed the corner a subdued exclamation was heard inside the wall.
'Ho – ho – Sergeant – ho – ho!' An expostulation followed, but it was indistinct; and it became lost amid a low peal of laughter, which was hardly distinguishable from the gurgle of the tiny whirlpools outside.

(Chapter 11)

Bathsheba and Sergeant Troy. (Original illustration by Helen Patterson Allingham in The Cornhill Magazine, *August 1874.)*

Sergeant Troy's first encounter with Bathsheba gives a new meaning to the phrase 'getting hitched'!

Her way back to the house was by a path through a young plantation of tapering firs, which had been planted some years earlier to shelter the premises from the north wind. By reason of the density of the interwoven foliage overhead it was gloomy there at cloudless noontide, twilight in the evening, dark as midnight at dusk, and black as the ninth plague of Egypt at midnight. To describe the spot is to call it a vast, low, naturally formed hall, the plumy ceiling of which was supported by slender pillars of living wood, the floor being covered with a soft dun carpet of dead spikelets and mildewed cones, with a tuft of grass-blades here and there.

This bit of the path was always the crux of the night's ramble, though, before starting, her apprehensions of danger were not vivid enough to lead her to take a companion. Slipping along here covertly as Time, Bathsheba fancied she could hear footsteps entering the track at the opposite end. It was certainly a rustle of footsteps. Her own instantly fell as gently as snowflakes. She reassured herself by a remembrance that the path was public, and that the traveller was probably some villager returning home; regretting, at the same time, that the meeting should be about to occur in the darkest point of her route, even though only just outside her own door.

The noise approached, came close, and a figure was apparently on the point of gliding past her when something tugged at her skirt and pinned it forcibly to the ground. The instantaneous check nearly threw Bathsheba off her balance. In recovering she struck against warm clothes and buttons.

'A rum start, upon my soul!' said a masculine voice, a foot or so above her head. 'Have I hurt you, mate?'

'No,' said Bathsheba, attempting to shrink away.

'We have got hitched together somehow, I think.'

'Yes.'

'Are you a woman?'

'Yes.'

'A lady, I should have said.'

'It doesn't matter.'

'I am a man.'

'Oh!'

Bathsheba softly tugged again, but to no purpose.

'Is that a dark lantern you have? I fancy so,' said the man.

'Yes.'

'If you'll allow me I'll open it, and set you free.'

A hand seized the lantern, the door was opened, the rays burst out from their prison, and Bathsheba beheld her position with astonishment.

The man to whom she was hooked was brilliant in brass and scarlet. He was a soldier. His sudden appearance was to darkness what the sound of a trumpet is to silence. The contrast of this revelation with her anticipations of some sinister figure in sombre garb was so great that it had upon her the effect of a fairy transformation.

It was immediately apparent that the military man's spur had become entangled in the gimp* which decorated the skirt of her dress. He caught a view of her face.

'I'll unfasten you in one moment, miss,' he said, with new-born gallantry.

'Oh no – I can do it, thank you,' she hastily replied, and stooped for the performance.

The unfastening was not such a trifling affair. The rowel* of the spur had so wound itself among the gimp cords in those few moments, that separation was likely to be a matter of time.

He too stooped, and the lantern standing on the ground betwixt them threw the gleam from its open side among the fir-tree needles and the blades of long damp grass with the effect of a large glow-worm. It radiated upwards into their faces, and sent over half the plantation gigantic shadows of both man and woman, each dusky shape becoming distorted and mangled upon the tree-trunks till it wasted to nothing.

He looked hard into her eyes when she raised them for a moment; Bathsheba looked down again, for his gaze was too strong to be received point-blank with her own. But she had obliquely noticed that he was young and slim, and that he wore three chevrons upon his sleeve.

Bathsheba pulled again.

'You are a prisoner, miss; it is no use blinking the matter,' said the soldier drily. 'I must cut your dress if you are in such a hurry.'

'Yes – please do!' she exclaimed helplessly.

'It wouldn't be necessary if you could wait a moment'; and he unwound a cord from the little wheel. She withdrew her own hand, but, whether by accident or design, he touched it. Bathsheba was vexed; she hardly knew why.

His unravelling went on, but it nevertheless seemed coming to no end. She looked at him again.

---

* gimp: a trimming made of silk or cotton with a cord or wire running through it

* rowel: the spiked wheel at the end of a spur

'Thank you for the sight of such a beautiful face!' said the young sergeant, without ceremony.

She coloured with embarrassment. ''Twas unwillingly shown,' she replied stiffly, and with as much dignity – which was very little – as she could infuse into a position of captivity.

'I like you the better for that incivility, miss,' he said.

'I should have liked – I wish – you had never shown yourself to me by intruding here!' She pulled again, and the gathers of her dress began to give way like lilliputian musketry.

'I deserve the chastisement your words give me. But why should such a fair and dutiful girl have such an aversion to her father's sex?'

'Go on your way, please.'

'What, Beauty, and drag you after me? Do but look; I never saw such a tangle!'

'Oh, 'tis shameful of you; you have been making it worse on purpose to keep me here – you have!'

'Indeed, I don't think so,' said the sergeant, with a merry twinkle.

'I tell you you have!' she exclaimed, in high temper. 'I insist upon undoing it. Now, allow me!'

'Certainly, miss; I am not of steel.' He added a sigh which had as much archness in it as a sigh could possess without losing its nature altogether. 'I am thankful for beauty, even when 'tis thrown to me like a bone to a dog. These moments will be over too soon!'

She closed her lips in a determined silence.

Bathsheba was revolving in her mind whether by a bold and desperate rush she could free herself at the risk of leaving her skirt bodily behind her. The thought was too dreadful. The dress – which she had put on to appear stately at the supper – was the head and front of her wardrobe; not another in her stock became her so well. What woman in Bathsheba's position, not naturally timid, and within call of her retainers, would have bought escape from a dashing soldier at so dear a price?

'All in good time; it will soon be done, I perceive,' said her cool friend.

'This trifling provokes, and – and –'

'Not too cruel!'

' – Insults me!'

'It is done in order that I may have the pleasure of apologizing to so charming a woman, which I straightway do most humbly, madam,' he said, bowing low.

Bathsheba really knew not what to say.

'I've seen a good many women in my time,' continued the young man in a murmur, and more thoughtfully than hitherto, critically regarding her bent head at the same time; 'but I've never seen a woman so beautiful as you. Take it or leave it – be offended or like it – I don't care.'

'Who are you, then, who can so well afford to despise opinion?'

'No stranger. Sergeant Troy. I am staying in this place. – There! it is undone at last, you see. Your light fingers were more eager than mine. I wish it had been the knot of knots, which there's no untying!'

This was worse and worse. She started up, and so did he. How to decently get away from him – that was her difficulty now. She sidled off inch by inch, the lantern in her hand, till she could see the redness of his coat no longer.

'Ah, Beauty; good-bye!' he said.

She made no reply, and, reaching a distance of twenty or thirty yards, turned about, and ran indoors.

(*Chapter 24*)

Far from the Madding Crowd

Bathsheba has already given Farmer Boldwood enough encouragement for him to believe there is a future in their relationship, but she has now become more interested in the dashing sergeant. Gabriel Oak, is anxious to advise her. He still loves her as much as when they had first met, although he knows he has 'lost in the race for money and good things'.

OAK determined to speak to his mistress. He would base his appeal on what he considered her unfair treatment of Farmer Boldwood, now absent from home.

An opportunity occurred one evening when she had gone for a short walk by a path through the neighbouring cornfields. It was dusk when Oak, who had not been far a-field that day, took the same path and met her returning, quite pensively, as he thought.

The wheat was now tall, and the path was narrow; thus the way was quite a sunken groove between the embowing thicket on either side. Two persons could not walk abreast without damaging the crop, and Oak stood aside to let her pass.

'Oh, is it Gabriel?' she said. 'You are taking a walk too. Good-night.'

'I thought I would come to meet you, as it is rather late,' said Oak, turning and following at her heels when she had brushed somewhat quickly by him.

'Thank you, indeed, but I am not very fearful.'

'Oh no; but there are bad characters about.'

'I never meet them.'

Now Oak, with marvellous ingenuity, had been going to introduce the gallant sergeant through the channel of 'bad characters'. But all at once the scheme broke down, it suddenly occurring to him that this was rather a clumsy way, and too barefaced to begin with. He tried another preamble.

'And as the man who would naturally come to meet you is away from home, too – I mean Farmer Boldwood – why, thinks I, I'll go,' he said.

'Ah, yes.' She walked on without turning her head, and for many steps nothing further was heard from her quarter than the rustle of her dress against the heavy corn-ears. Then she resumed rather tartly –

'I don't quite understand what you meant by saying that Mr. Boldwood would naturally come to meet me.'

'I meant on account of the wedding which they say is likely to take place between you and him, miss. Forgive my speaking plainly.'

'They say what is not true,' she returned quickly. 'No marriage is likely to take place between us.'

Gabriel now put forth his unobscured opinion, for the moment had come. 'Well, Miss Everdene,' he said, 'putting aside what people say, I never in my life saw any courting if his is not a courting of you.'

Bathsheba would probably have terminated the conversation there and then by flatly forbidding the subject, had not her conscious weakness of position allured her to palter and argue in endeavours to better it.

'Since this subject has been mentioned,' she said very emphatically, 'I am glad of the opportunity of clearing up a mistake which is very common and very provoking. I didn't definitely promise Mr. Boldwood anything. I have never cared for him. I respect him, and he has urged me to marry him. But I have given him no distinct answer. As soon as he returns I shall do so; and the answer will be that I cannot think of marrying him.'

'People are full of mistakes, seemingly.'

'They are.'

'The other day they said you were trifling with him, and you almost proved that you were not; lately they have said that you be not, and you straightway begin to show—'

'That I am, I suppose you mean.'

'Well, I hope they speak the truth.'

'They do, but wrongly applied. I don't trifle with him; but then, I have nothing to do with him.'

Oak was unfortunately led on to speak of Boldwood's rival in a wrong tone to her after all. 'I wish you had never met that young Sergeant Troy, miss,' he sighed.

Bathsheba's steps became faintly spasmodic. 'Why?' she asked.

'He is not good enough for 'ee.'

'Did any one tell you to speak to me like this?'

'Nobody at all.'

'Then it appears to me that Sergeant Troy does not concern us here,' she said intractably. 'Yet I must say that Sergeant Troy is an educated man, and quite worthy of any woman. He is well born.'

'His being higher in learning and birth than the ruck* o' soldiers is anything but a proof of his worth. It shows his course to be down'ard.'

'I cannot see what this has to do with our conversation. Mr. Troy's course is not by any means downward; and his superiority *is* a proof of his worth!'

'I believe him to have no conscience at all. And I cannot help begging you, miss, to have nothing to do with him. Listen to me this once – only this once! I don't say he's such a bad man as I have fancied – I pray to God he is not. But since we don't exactly know what he is, why not behave as if he *might* be bad, simply for your own safety? Don't trust him,

---

* ruck: the general run; the 'common herd'

mistress; I ask you not to trust him so.'

'Why, pray?'

'I like soldiers, but this one I do not like,' he said sturdily. 'His cleverness in his calling may have tempted him astray, and what is mirth to the neighbours is ruin to the woman. When he tries to talk to 'ee again, why not turn away with a short "Good day"; and when you see him coming one way, turn the other. When he says anything laughable, fail to see the point and don't smile, and speak of him before those who will report your talk as "that fantastical man", or "that Sergeant What's-his-name". "That man of a family that has come to the dogs." Don't be unmannerly towards en, but harmless-uncivil, and so get rid of the man.'

No Christmas robin detained by a window-pane ever pulsed as did Bathsheba now.

'I say – I say again – that it doesn't become you to talk about him. Why he should be mentioned passes me quite!' she exclaimed desperately. 'I know this, th-th-that he is a thoroughly conscientious man – blunt sometimes even to rudeness – but always speaking his mind about you plain to your face!'

'Oh.'

'He is as good as anybody in this parish! He is very particular, too, about going to church – yes, he is!'

'I am afeard nobody ever saw him there. I never did, certainly.'

'The reason of that is,' she said eagerly, 'that he goes in privately by the old tower door, just when the service commences, and sits at the back of the gallery. He told me so.'

This supreme instance of Troy's goodness fell upon Gabriel's ears like the thirteenth stroke of a crazy clock. It was not only received with utter incredulity as regarded itself, but threw a doubt on all the assurances that had preceded it.

Oak was grieved to find how entirely she trusted him. He brimmed with deep feeling as he replied in a steady voice, the steadiness of which was spoilt by the palpableness of his great effort to keep it so: –

'You know, mistress, that I love you, and shall love you always. I only mention this to bring to your mind that at any rate I would wish to do you no harm: beyond that I put it aside. I have lost in the race for money and good things, and I am not such a fool as to pretend to 'ee now I am poor, and you have got altogether above me. But Bathsheba, dear mistress, this I beg you to consider – that, both to keep yourself well honoured among the workfolk, and in common generosity to an honourable man who loves you as well as I, you should be more discreet in your bearing towards this soldier.'

'Don't, don't, don't!' she exclaimed, in a choking voice.

(*Chapter 29*)

Boldwood, still hoping that Bathsheba will be his, confronts Troy with a proposition.

Boldwood did not hurry homeward. It was ten o'clock at least, when, walking deliberately through the lower part of Weatherbury, he heard the carrier's spring van entering the village. The van ran to and from a town in a northern direction, and it was owned and driven by a Weatherbury man, at the door of whose house it now pulled up. The lamp fixed to the head of the hood illuminated a scarlet and gilded form, who was the first to alight.

'Ah!' said Boldwood to himself, 'come to see her again.'

Troy entered the carrier's house, which had been the place of his lodging on his last visit to his native place. Boldwood was moved by a sudden determination. He hastened home. In ten minutes he was back again, and made as if he were going to call upon Troy at the carrier's. But as he approached, some one opened the door and came out. He heard this person say 'Good-night' to the inmates, and the voice was Troy's. This was strange, coming so immediately after his arrival. Boldwood, however, hastened up to him. Troy had what appeared to be a carpet-bag in his hand – the same that he had brought with him. It seemed as if he were going to leave again this very night.

Troy turned up the hill and quickened his pace. Boldwood stepped forward.

'Sergeant Troy?'

'Yes – I'm Sergeant Troy.'

'Just arrived from up the country, I think?'

'Just arrived from Bath.'

'I am William Boldwood.'

'Indeed.'

The tone in which this word was uttered was all that had been wanted to bring Boldwood to the point.

'I wish to speak a word with you,' he said.

'What about?'

'About her who lives just ahead there – and about a woman you have wronged.'

'I wonder at your impertinence,' said Troy, moving on.

'Now look here,' said Boldwood, standing in front of him, 'wonder or not, you are going to hold a conversation with me.'

Troy heard the dull determination in Boldwood's voice, looked at his stalwart frame, then at the thick cudgel he carried in his hand. He remembered it was past ten o'clock. It seemed worth while to be civil to Boldwood.

'Very well, I'll listen with pleasure,' said Troy, placing his bag on the ground, 'only speak low, for somebody or other may overhear us in the farmhouse there.'

'Well then – I know a good deal concerning your – Fanny Robin's attachment to you. I may say, too, that I believe I am the only person in the village, excepting Gabriel Oak, who does know it. You ought to marry her.'

'I suppose I ought. Indeed, I wish to, but I cannot.'

'Why?'

Troy was about to utter something hastily; he then checked himself and said, 'I am too poor.' His voice was changed. Previously it had had a devil-may-care tone. It was the voice of a trickster now.

Boldwood's present mood was not critical enough to notice tones. He continued, 'I may as well speak plainly; and understand, I don't wish to enter into the questions of right or wrong, woman's honour and shame, or to express any opinion on your conduct. I intend a business transaction with you.'

'I see,' said Troy. 'Suppose we sit down here.'

An old tree trunk lay under the hedge immediately opposite, and they sat down.

'I was engaged to be married to Miss Everdene,' said Boldwood, 'but you came and—'

'Not engaged,' said Troy.

'As good as engaged.'

'If I had not turned up she might have become engaged to you.'

'Hang might!'

'Would, then.'

'If you had not come I should certainly – yes, *certainly* – have been accepted by this time. If you had not seen her you might have been married to Fanny. Well, there's too much difference between Miss Everdene's station and your own for this flirtation with her ever to benefit you by ending in marriage. So all I ask is, don't molest her any more. Marry Fanny. I'll make it worth your while.'

'How will you?'

'I'll pay you well now, I'll settle a sum of money upon her, and I'll see that you don't suffer from poverty in the future. I'll put it clearly. Bathsheba is only playing with you: you are too poor for her as I said; so give up wasting your time about a great match you'll never make for a moderate and rightful match you may make to-morrow; take up your carpet-bag, turn about, leave Weatherbury now, this night, and you shall take fifty pounds with you. Fanny shall have fifty to enable her to prepare for the wedding, when you have told me where she is living, and she shall have five hundred paid down on her wedding-day.'

In making this statement Boldwood's voice revealed only too clearly a consciousness of the weakness of his position, his aims, and his method. His manner had lapsed quite from that of the firm and dignified Boldwood of former times; and such a scheme as he had now engaged in he would have condemned as childishly imbecile only a few months ago. We discern a grand force in the lover which he lacks whilst a free man; but there is a breadth of vision in the free man which in the lover we vainly seek. Where there is much bias there must be some narrowness, and love, though added emotion, is subtracted capacity. Boldwood exemplified this to an abnormal degree: he knew nothing of Fanny Robin's circumstances or whereabouts, he knew nothing of Troy's possibilities, yet that was what he said.

'I like Fanny best,' said Troy; 'and if, as you say, Miss Everdene is out of my reach, why I have all to gain by accepting your money, and marrying Fan. But she's only a servant.'

'Never mind – do you agree to my arrangement?'

'I do.'

'Ah!' said Boldwood, in a more elastic voice. 'Oh, Troy, if you like her best, why then did you step in here and injure my happiness?'

'I love Fanny best now,' said Troy. 'But Bathsh – Miss Everdene inflamed me, and displaced Fanny for a time. It is over now.'

'Why should it be over so soon? And why then did you come here again?'

'There are weighty reasons. Fifty pounds at once, you said!'

'I did,' said Boldwood, 'and here they are – fifty sovereigns.' He handed Troy a small packet.

'You have everything ready – it seems that you calculated on my accepting them,' said the sergeant, taking the packet.

'I thought you might accept them,' said Boldwood.

'You've only my word that the programme shall be adhered to, whilst I at any rate have fifty pounds.'

'I had thought of that, and I have considered that if I can't appeal to your honour I can trust to your – well, shrewdness we'll call it – not to lose five hundred pounds in prospect, and also make a bitter enemy of a man who is willing to be an extremely useful friend.'

'Stop, listen!' said Troy in a whisper.

A light pit-pat was audible upon the road just above them.

'By George – 'tis she,' he continued. 'I must go on and meet her.'

'She – who?'

'Bathsheba.'

'Bathsheba – out alone at this time o' night!' said Boldwood in amazement, and starting up. 'Why must you meet her?'

'She was expecting me to-night – and I must now speak to her, and wish her good-bye, according to your wish.'

'I don't see the necessity of speaking.'

'It can do no harm – and she'll be wandering about looking for me if I don't. You shall hear all I say to her. It will help you in your love-making when I am gone.'

'Your tone is mocking.'

'Oh no. And remember this, if she does not know what has become of me, she will think more about me than if I tell her flatly I have come to give her up.'

'Will you confine your words to that one point? – Shall I hear every word you say?'

'Every word. Now sit still there, and hold my carpet-bag for me, and mark what you hear.'

The light footstep came closer, halting occasionally, as if the walker listened for a sound. Troy whistled a double note in a soft, fluty tone.

'Come to that, is it!' murmured Boldwood uneasily.

'You promised silence,' said Troy.

'I promise again.'

Troy stepped forward.

'Frank, dearest, is that you?' The tones were Bathsheba's.

'Oh God!' said Boldwood.

'Yes,' said Troy to her.

'How late you are,' she continued tenderly. 'Did you come by the carrier? I listened and heard his wheels entering the village, but it was some time ago, and I had almost given you up, Frank.'

'I was sure to come,' said Frank. 'You knew I should, did you not?'

'Well, I thought you would,' she said playfully; 'and, Frank, it is so lucky! There's not a soul in my house but me to-night. I've packed them all off, so nobody on earth will know of your visit to your lady's bower. Liddy wanted to go to her grandfather's to tell him about her holiday, and I said she might stay with them till to-morrow – when you'll be gone again.'

'Capital,' said Troy. 'But, dear me, I had better go back for my bag, because my slippers and brush and comb are in it; you run home whilst I fetch it, and I'll promise to be in your parlour in ten minutes.'

'Yes.' She turned and tripped up the hill again.

During the progress of this dialogue there was a nervous twitching of Boldwood's tightly closed lips, and his face became bathed in a clammy dew. He now started forward towards Troy. Troy turned to him and took up the bag.

'There's not a soul in my house but me to-night.' (see page 31). (Original illustration by Helen Patterson Allingham in The Cornhill Magazine, *August 1874.)*

'Shall I tell her I have come to give her up and cannot marry her?' said the soldier mockingly.

'No, no; wait a minute. I want to say more to you – more to you!' said Boldwood, in a hoarse whisper.

'Now,' said Troy, 'you see my dilemma. Perhaps I am a bad man – the victim of my impulses – led away to do what I ought to leave undone. I can't, however, marry them both. And I have two reasons for choosing. Fanny. First, I like her best upon the whole, and second, you make it worth my while.'

At the same instant Boldwood sprang upon him, and held him by the neck. Troy felt Boldwood's grasp slowly tightening. The move was absolutely unexpected.

'A moment,' he gasped. 'You are injuring her you love!'

'Well, what do you mean?' said the farmer.

'Give me breath,' said Troy.

Boldwood loosened his hand, saying, 'By Heaven, I've a mind to kill you!'

'And ruin her.'

'Save her.'

'Oh, how can she be saved now, unless I marry her?'

Boldwood groaned. He reluctantly released the soldier, and flung him back against the hedge. 'Devil, you torture me!' said he.

Troy rebounded like a ball, and was about to make a dash at the farmer; but he checked himself, saying lightly: –

'It is not worth while to measure my strength with you. Indeed it is a barbarous way of settling a quarrel. I shall shortly leave the army because of the same conviction. Now after that revelation of how the land lies with Bathsheba, 'twould be a mistake to kill me, would it not?'

''Twould be a mistake to kill you,' repeated Boldwood, mechanically, with a bowed head.

'Better kill yourself.'

'Far better.'

'I'm glad you see it.'

'Troy, make her your wife, and don't act upon what I arranged just now. The alternative is dreadful, but take Bathsheba; I give her up! She must love you indeed to sell soul and body to you so utterly as she has done. Wretched woman – deluded woman – you are, Bathsheba!'

'But about Fanny?'

'Bathsheba is a woman well to do,' continued Boldwood, in nervous anxiety, 'and, Troy, she will make a good wife; and, indeed, she is worth your hastening on your marriage with her!'

'But she has a will – not to say a temper, and I shall be a mere slave to her. I could do anything with poor Fanny Robin.'

'Troy,' said Boldwood imploringly, 'I'll do anything for you, only don't desert her; pray don't desert her, Troy.'

'Which, poor Fanny?'

'No; Bathsheba Everdene. Love her best! Love her tenderly! How shall I get you to see how advantageous it will be to you to secure her at once?'

'I don't wish to secure her in any new way.'

Boldwood's arm moved spasmodically towards Troy's person again. He repressed the instinct, and his form drooped as with pain.

Troy went on: –

'I shall soon purchase my discharge, and then—'

'But I wish you to hasten on this marriage! It will be better for you both. You love each other, and you must let me help you to do it.'

'How?'

'Why, by settling the five hundred on Bathsheba instead of Fanny, to enable you to marry at once. No; she wouldn't have it of me. I'll pay it down to you on the wedding-day.'

Troy paused in secret amazement at Boldwood's wild infatuation. He carelessly said, 'And am I to have anything now?'

'Yes, if you wish to. But I have not much additional money with me. I did not expect this; but all I have is yours.'

Boldwood, more like a somnambulist than a wakeful man, pulled out the large canvas bag he carried by way of a purse, and searched it.

'I have twenty-one pounds more with me,' he said. 'Two notes and a sovereign. But before I leave you I must have a paper signed—'

'Pay me the money, and we'll go straight to her parlour, and make any arrangement you please to secure my compliance with your wishes. But she must know nothing of this cash business.'

'Nothing, nothing,' said Boldwood hastily. 'Here is the sum, and if you'll come to my house we'll write out the agreement for the remainder, and the terms also.'

'First we'll call upon her.'

'But why? Come with me to-night, and go with me to-morrow to the surrogate's.'*

'But she must be consulted; at any rate informed.'

'Very well; go on.'

They went up the hill to Bathsheba's house. When they stood at the entrance, Troy said, 'Wait here a moment.' Opening the door, he glided inside, leaving the door ajar.

Boldwood waited. In two minutes a light appeared in the passage. Boldwood then saw that the chain had been fastened across the door. Troy appeared inside carrying a bedroom candlestick.

---

* surrogate: a bishop's deputy for granting marriage licences

'What, did you think I should break in?' said Boldwood contemptuously.

'Oh, no; it is merely my humour to secure things. Will you read this a moment? I'll hold the light.'

Troy handed a folded newspaper through the slit between door and door-post, and put the candle close. 'That's the paragraph,' he said, placing his finger on a line.

Boldwood looked and read

MARRIAGES

'On the 17th inst., at St. Ambrose's Church, Bath, by the Rev. G. Mincing, B.A., Francis Troy, only son of the late Edward Troy, Esq., M.D., of Weatherbury, and sergeant 11th Dragoon Guards, to Bathsheba, only surviving daughter of the late Mr. John Everdene, of Casterbridge.'

(Chapter 34)

Boldwood is giving a Christmas party where he is trying to persuade Bathsheba to wear his ring, believing that her husband, Troy, has been lost at sea.

Boldwood had come close to her side, and now he clasped one of her hands in both his own, and lifted it to his breast.

'What is it? Oh I cannot wear a ring!' she exclaimed, on seeing what he held; 'besides, I wouldn't have a soul know that it's an engagement! Perhaps it is improper? Besides, we are not engaged in the usual sense, are we? Don't insist, Mr. Boldwood – don't!' In her trouble at not being able to get her hand away from him at once, she stamped passionately on the floor with one foot, and tears crowded to her eyes again.

'It means simply a pledge – no sentiment – the seal of a practical compact,' he said more quietly, but still retaining her hand in his firm grasp. 'Come, now!' And Boldwood slipped the ring on her finger.

'I cannot wear it,' she said, weeping as if her heart would break. 'You frighten me, almost. So wild a scheme! Please let me go home!'

'Only to-night: wear it just to-night, to please me!'

Bathsheba sat down in a chair, and buried her face in her handkerchief, though Boldwood kept her hand yet. At length she said, in a sort of hopeless whisper: –

'Very well, then, I will to-night, if you wish it so earnestly. Now loosen my hand; I will, indeed I will wear it to-night.'

'And it shall be the beginning of a pleasant secret courtship of six years, with a wedding at the end?'

'It must be, I suppose, since you will have it so!' she said, fairly beaten into non-resistance.

Boldwood pressed her hand, and allowed it to drop in her lap. 'I am happy now,' he said. 'God bless you!'

He left the room, and when he thought she might be sufficiently composed sent one of the maids to her. Bathsheba cloaked the effects of the late scene as she best could, followed the girl, and in a few moments came downstairs with her hat and cloak on, ready to go. To get to the door it was necessary to pass through the hall, and before doing so she paused on the bottom of the staircase which descended into one corner, to take a last look at the gathering.

There was no music or dancing in progress just now. At the lower end, which had been arranged for the work-folk specially, a group conversed in whispers, and with clouded looks. Boldwood was standing by the fireplace, and he, too, though so absorbed in visions arising from her promise that he scarcely saw anything, seemed at that moment to have observed their peculiar manner, and their looks askance.

'What is it you are in doubt about, men?' he said.

One of them turned and replied uneasily: 'It was something Laban heard of, that's all, sir.'

'News? Anybody married or engaged, born or dead?' inquired the farmer, gaily. 'Tell it to us, Tall. One would think from your looks and mysterious ways that it was something very dreadful indeed.'

'Oh no, sir, nobody is dead,' said Tall.

'I wish somebody was,' said Samway, in a whisper.

'What do you say, Samway?' asked Boldwood, somewhat sharply. 'If you have anything to say, speak out; if not, get up another dance.'

'Mrs. Troy has come downstairs,' said Samway to Tall. 'If you want to tell her, you had better do it now.'

'Do you know what they mean?' the farmer asked Bathsheba, across the room.

'I don't in the least,' said Bathsheba.

There was a smart rapping at the door. One of the men opened it instantly, and went outside.

'Mrs. Troy is wanted,' he said, on returning.

'Quite ready,' said Bathsheba. 'Though I didn't tell them to send.'

'It is a stranger, ma'am,' said the man by the door.

'A stranger?' she said.

'Ask him to come in,' said Boldwood.

The message was given, and Troy, wrapped up to his eyes as we have seen him, stood in the doorway.

There was an unearthly silence, all looking towards the newcomer. Those who had just learnt that he was in the neighbourhood recognized him instantly; those who did not were perplexed. Nobody noted Bathsheba. She was leaning on the stairs. Her brow had heavily contracted; her whole face was pallid, her lips apart, her eyes rigidly staring at their visitor.

Boldwood was among those who did not notice that he was Troy. 'Come in, come in!' he repeated, cheerfully, 'and drain a Christmas beaker with us, stranger!'

Troy next advanced into the middle of the room, took off his cap, turned down his coat-collar, and looked Boldwood in the face. Even then Boldwood did not recognize that the impersonator of Heaven's persistent irony towards him, who had once before broken in upon his bliss, scourged him, and snatched his delight away, had come to do these things a second time. Troy began to laugh a mechanical laugh: Boldwood recognized him now.

Troy turned to Bathsheba. The poor girl's wretchedness at this time

Troy next advanced into the middle of the room, took off his cap... (see page 37). (Original illustration by Helen Patterson Allingham in The Cornhill Magazine, *December 1874.)*

was beyond all fancy or narration. She had sunk down on the lowest stair; and there she sat, her mouth blue and dry, and her dark eyes fixed vacantly upon him, as if she wondered whether it were not all a terrible illusion.

Then Troy spoke. 'Bathsheba, I come here for you!'
She made no reply.
'Come home with me: come!'
Bathsheba moved her feet a little, but did not rise.
Troy went across to her.
'Come, madam, do you hear what I say?' he said, peremptorily.
A strange voice came from the fireplace – a voice sounding far off and confined, as if from a dungeon. Hardly a soul in the assembly recognized

the thin tones to be those of Boldwood. Sudden despair had transformed him.

'Bathsheba, go with your husband!'

Troy stretched out his hand to pull her towards him, when she quickly shrank back. This visible dread of him seemed to irritate Troy, and he seized her arm and pulled it sharply. Whether his grasp pinched her, or whether his mere touch was the cause, was never known, but at the moment of his seizure she writhed, and gave a quick, low scream.

The scream had been heard but a few seconds when it was followed by a sudden deafening report that echoed through the room and stupefied them all. The oak partition shook with the concussion, and the place was filled with grey smoke.

In bewilderment they turned their eyes to Boldwood. At his back, as he stood before the fireplace, was a gun-rack, as is usual in farmhouses, constructed to hold two guns. When Bathsheba had cried out in her husband's grasp, Boldwood's face of gnashing despair had changed. The veins had swollen, and a frenzied look had gleamed in his eye. He had turned quickly, taken one of the guns, cocked it, and at once discharged it at Troy.

Troy fell. The distance apart of the two men was so small that the charge of shot did not spread in the least, but passed like a bullet into his body. He uttered a long guttural sigh – there was a contraction – an extension – then his muscles relaxed, and he lay still.

Boldwood was seen through the smoke to be now again engaged with the gun. It was double-barrelled, and he had, meanwhile, in some way fastened his handkerchief to the trigger, and with his foot on the other end was in the act of turning the second barrel upon himself. Samway his man was the first to see this, and in the midst of the general horror darted up to him. Boldwood had already twitched the handkerchief, and the gun exploded a second time, sending its contents, by a timely blow from Samway, into the beam which crossed the ceiling.

'Well, it makes no difference!' Boldwood gasped. 'There is another way for me to die.'

Then he broke from Samway, crossed the room to Bathsheba, and kissed her hand. He put on his hat, opened the door, and went into the darkness, nobody thinking of preventing him.

(Chapter 53)

In the final four chapters of the novel Hardy brings the hitherto tangled plot to a neat and happy ending.

The Vampirine Fair

Gilbert had sailed to India's shore,
  And I was all alone:
My lord came in at my open door
  And said, 'O fairest one'.

He leant upon the slant bureau,
  And sighed, 'I am sick for thee!'
'My Lord,' said I, 'pray speak not so,
  Since wedded wife I be.'

Leaning upon the slant bureau,
  Bitter his next words came:
'So much I know; and likewise know
  My love burns on the same!

'But since you thrust my love away,
  And since it knows no cure,
I must live out as best I may
  The ache that I endure.'

When Michaelmas browned the nether Coomb,
  And Wingreen Hill above,
And made the hollyhocks rags of bloom,
  My lord grew ill of love.

My lord grew ill with love for me;
  Gilbert was far from port;
And – so it was – that time did see
  Me housed at Manor Court.

About the bowers of Manor Court
  The primrose pushed its head
When, on a day at last, report
  Arrived of him I had wed.

'Gilbert, my Lord, is homeward bound,
  His sloop is drawing near,
What shall I do when I am found
  Not in his house but here?'

'O I will heal the injuries
  I've done to him and thee.
I'll give him means to live at ease
  Afar from Shastonb'ry.'

When Gilbert came we both took thought:
  'Since comfort and good cheer,'
Said he, 'so readily are bought,
  He's welcome to thee, Dear.'

So when my lord flung liberally
  His gold in Gilbert's hands,
I coaxed and got my brothers three
  Made stewards of his lands.

And then I coaxed him to install
  My other kith and kin,
With aim to benefit them all
  Before his love ran thin.

And next I craved to be possessed
  Of plate and jewels rare.
He groaned: 'You give me, Love, no rest,
  Take all the law will spare!'

And so in course of years my wealth
  Became a goodly hoard,
My steward brethren, too, by stealth
  Had each a fortune stored.

Thereafter in the gloom he'd walk,
  And by and by began
To say aloud in absent talk,
  'I am a ruined man! –

'I hardly could have thought,' he said,
  'When first I looked on thee,
That one so soft, so rosy red,
  Could thus have beggared me!'

Seeing his fair estates in pawn,
   And him in such decline,
I knew that his domain had gone
   To lift up me and mine.

Next month upon a Sunday morn
   A gunshot sounded nigh:
By his own hand my lordly born
   Had doomed himself to die.

'Live, my dear Lord, and much of thine
   Shall be restored to thee!'
He smiled, and said 'twixt word and sign,
   'Alas – that cannot be!'

And while I searched his cabinet
   For letters, keys, or will,
'Twas touching that his gaze was set
   With love upon me still.

And when I burnt each document
   Before his dying eyes,
'Twas sweet that he did not resent
   My fear of compromise.

The steeple-cock gleamed golden when
   I watched his spirit go:
And I became repentant then
   That I had wrecked him so.

Three weeks at least had come and gone,
   With many a saddened word,
Before I wrote to Gilbert on
   The stroke that so had stirred.

And having worn a mournful gown,
   I joined, in decent while,
My husband at a dashing town
   To live in dashing style.

Yet though I now enjoy my fling,
   And dine and dance and drive,
I'd give my prettiest emerald ring
   To see my lord alive.

And when the meet on hunting-days
   Is near his churchyard home,
I leave my bantering beaux to place
   A flower upon his tomb;

And sometimes say: 'Perhaps too late
   The saints in Heaven deplore
That tender time when, moved by Fate,
   He darked my cottage door.'

Stinsford Church – the church closest to his birthplace and most frequently visited by Hardy. He regularly visited Stinsford in his old age because his parents, sister and first wife were buried there. Hardy's heart was buried in this churchyard.

At a Watering-Place

They sit and smoke on the esplanade,
   The man and his friend, and regard the bay
Where the far chalk cliffs, to the left displayed,
Smile sallowly in the decline of day.
And saunterers pass with laugh and jest –
A handsome couple among the rest.

'That smart proud pair,' says the man to his friend,
'Are to marry next week. . . . How little he thinks
That dozens of days and nights on end
I have stroked her neck, unhooked the links
Of her sleeve to get at her upper arm. . . .
Well, bliss is in ignorance: what's the harm!'

The Dark-Eyed Gentleman

I

I PITCHED my day's leazings* in Crimmercrock Lane,
To tie up my garter and jog on again,
When a dear dark-eyed gentleman passed there and said,
In a way that made all o' me colour rose-red,
    'What do I see –
    O pretty knee!'
And he came and he tied up my garter for me!

II

'Twixt sunset and moonrise it was, I can mind:
Ah, 'tis easy to lose what we nevermore find! –
Of the dear stranger's home, of his name, I knew nought,
But I soon knew his nature and all that it brought.
    Then bitterly
    Sobbed I that he
Should ever have tied up my garter for me!

III

Yet now I've beside me a fine lissom lad,
And my slip's nigh forgot, and my days are not sad;
My own dearest joy is he, comrade, and friend,
He it is who safe-guards me, on him I depend;
    No sorrow brings he,
    And thankful I be
That his daddy once tied up my garter for me!

---

* leazings: bundle of gleaned corn

The furmity woman at Weydon-Priors fair (see page 47). (Original illustration by Robert Barnes in The Graphic, *9 January 1886.)*

The Mayor of Casterbridge

Michael Henchard: his rise and fall

The novel first appeared in serial form in 20 instalments in **The Graphic** between 2 January and 15 May 1886. Not all reviews were favourable:

'It is a fiction stranger than truth; for even at the comparatively distant date — some fifty years ago — when and where the scenes are laid, it is impossible to believe that the public sale by a husband of his wife and child to a sailor, in a crowded booth at a village fair, could have attracted such slight attention from the many onlookers.... Again, is it possible that Michael Henchard, so thoroughly selfish and unprincipled when young, could have been refined by a temperance vow... into a man of considerable delicacy, honour and generosity?'

(**The Saturday Review**, 29 May 1886)

Michael Henchard, a poor hay-trusser, in a rash moment of drunkenness, sells his wife to a sailor for five guineas. They walk off to a new life leaving Henchard to repent and swear an oath not to drink alcohol for twenty one years — being his age at the time.

Having lost his family, he moves on and settles in Casterbridge, where he soon finds fame and fortune as a man of business and influence. He employs men in his corn merchant's business, including a young Scotsman, Donald Farfrae, a newcomer to Casterbridge, who eventually usurps Henchard's prominent position in the town. At the same time, Farfrae becomes more than a little emotionally involved with the women in Henchard's life.

The Mayor of Casterbridge

The first extract, taken from Chapter 28, illustrates one of the ways in which Henchard's past catches up with him.

THE NEXT morning Henchard went to the Town Hall below Lucetta's* house, to attend Petty Sessions, being still a magistrate for the year by virtue of his late position as Mayor. In passing he looked up at windows, but nothing of her was to be seen.

Henchard as a Justice of the Peace may at first seem to be an even greater incongruity than Shallow and Silence* themselves. But his rough and ready perceptions, his sledgehammer directness, had often served him better than nice legal knowledge in despatching such simple business as fell to his hands in this Court. To-day Dr. Chalkfield, the Mayor for the year, being absent, the corn-merchant took the big chair, his eyes still abstractedly stretching out of the window to the ashlar front of High-Place Hall.

There was one case only, and the offender stood before him. She was an old woman of mottled countenance, attired in a shawl of that nameless tertiary hue which comes, but cannot be made – a hue neither tawny, russet, hazel, nor ash; a sticky black bonnet that seemed to have been worn in the country of the Psalmist where the clouds drop fatness; and an apron that had been white in times so comparatively recent as still to contrast visibly with the rest of her clothes. The steeped aspect of the woman as a whole showed her to be no native of the country-side or even of a country-town.

She looked cursorily at Henchard and the second magistrate, and Henchard looked at her, with a momentary pause, as if she had reminded him indistinctly of somebody or something which passed from his mind as quickly as it had come. 'Well, and what has she been doing?' he said, looking down at the charge-sheet.

'She is charged, sir, with the offence of disorderly female and nuisance,' whispered Stubberd.

'Where did she do that?' said the other magistrate.

'By the church, sir, of all the horrible places in the world! – I caught her in the act, your worship.'

'Stand back then,' said Henchard, 'and let's hear what you've got to say.'

Stubberd was sworn, the magistrate's clerk dipped his pen, Henchard being no note-taker himself, and the constable began –

---

* Lucetta: a newcomer to Casterbridge, whom Henchard hopes to marry
* Shallow and Silence: two comic magistrates in Shakespeare's *Henry IV Part 2*

'Hearing a' illegal noise I went down the street at twenty-five minutes past eleven P.M. on the night of the fifth instinct, Hannah Dominy. When I had—'

'Don't go on so fast, Stubberd,' said the clerk.

The constable waited, with his eyes on the clerk's pen, till the latter stopped scratching and said, 'yes.' Stubberd continued: 'When I had proceeded to the spot I saw defendant at another spot, namely, the gutter.' He paused, watching the point of the clerk's pen again.

'Gutter, yes, Stubberd.'

'Spot measuring twelve feet nine inches or thereabouts, from where I—' Still careful not to outrun the clerk's penmanship Stubberd pulled up again; for having got his evidence by heart it was immaterial to him whereabouts he broke off.

'I object to that,' spoke up the old woman, ' "spot measuring twelve feet nine or thereabouts from where I," is not sound testimony!'

The magistrates consulted, and the second one said that the bench was of opinion that twelve feet nine inches from a man on his oath was admissible.

Stubberd, with a suppressed gaze of victorious rectitude at the old woman, continued: 'Was standing myself. She was wambling* about quite dangerous to the thoroughfare, and when I approached to draw near she committed the nuisance, and insulted me.'

' "Insulted me." . . . Yes, what did she say?'

'She said, "Put away that dee lantern," she says.'

'Yes.'

'Says she, "Dost hear, old turmit-head?* Put away that dee lantern. I have floored fellows a dee sight finer-looking than a dee fool like thee, you son of a bee, dee me if I haint," she says.'

'I object to that conversation!' interposed the old woman. 'I was not capable enough to hear what I said, and what is said out of my hearing is not evidence.'

There was another stoppage for consultation, a book was referred to, and finally Stubberd was allowed to go on again. The truth was that the old woman had appeared in court so many more times than the magistrates themselves, that they were obliged to keep a sharp look-out upon their procedure. However, when Stubberd had rambled on a little further Henchard broke out impatiently, 'Come – we don't want to hear any more of them cust dees and bees! Say the words out like a man, and don't be so modest, Stubberd; or else leave it alone!' Turning to the woman, 'Now then, have you any questions to ask him, or anything to say?'

* wambling: tottering
* turmit-head: turnip-head; scarecrow; idiot

'Yes,' she replied with a twinkle in her eye; and the clerk dipped his pen.

'Twenty years ago or thereabouts I was selling of furmity in a tent at Weydon Fair—'

' "Twenty years ago" – well, that's beginning at the beginning; suppose you go back to the Creation!' said the clerk, not without satire.

But Henchard stared, and quite forgot what was evidence and what was not.

'A man and a woman with a little child came into my tent,' the woman continued. 'They sat down and had a basin apiece. Ah, Lord's my life! I was of a more respectable station in the world then than I am now, being a land smuggler in a large way of business; and I used to season my furmity with rum for them who asked for't. I did it for the man; and then he had more and more; till at last he quarrelled with his wife, and offered to sell her to the highest bidder. A sailor came in and bid five guineas, and paid the money, and led her away. And the man who sold his wife in that fashion is the man sitting there in the great big chair.' The speaker concluded by nodding her head at Henchard and folding her arms.

Everybody looked at Henchard. His face seemed strange, and in tint as if it had been powdered over with ashes. 'We don't want to hear your life and adventures,' said the second magistrate sharply, filling the pause which followed. 'You've been asked if you've anything to say bearing on the case.'

'That bears on the case. It proves that he's no better than I, and has no right to sit there in judgment upon me.'

''Tis a concocted story,' said the clerk. 'So hold your tongue!'

'No – 'tis true.' The words came from Henchard. ''Tis as true as the light,' he said slowly. 'And upon my soul it does prove that I'm no better than she! And to keep out of any temptation to treat her hard for her revenge, I'll leave her to you.'

The sensation in the court was indescribably great. Henchard left the chair, and came out, passing through a group of people on the steps and outside that was much larger than usual; for it seemed that the old furmity dealer had mysteriously hinted to the denizens of the lane in which she had been lodging since her arrival, that she knew a queer thing or two about their great local man Mr. Henchard, if she chose to tell it. This had brought them hither.

'Why are there so many idlers round the Town Hall to-day?' said Lucetta to her servant when the case was over. She had risen late, and had just looked out of the window.

'Oh, please, ma'am, 'tis this larry* about Mr. Henchard. A woman

---

* larry: commotion

has proved that before he became a gentleman he sold his wife for five guineas in a booth at a fair.'

In all the accounts which Henchard had given her of the separation from his wife Susan for so many years, of his belief in her death, and so on, he had never clearly explained the actual and immediate cause of that separation. The story she now heard for the first time.

(Chapter 28)

'Any trade doing here?' he asked . . . (see page 52). (Original illustration by Robert Barnes in The Graphic, *2 January 1886.)*

Because so much of what happens in the novel stems from and refers back to the wife-selling incident, it is worth going back in the novel and reading the account of the episode in the opening chapter.

ONE EVENING of late summer, before the nineteenth century had reached one-third of its span, a young man and woman, the latter carrying a child, were approaching the large village of Weydon-Priors, in Upper Wessex, on foot. They were plainly but not ill clad, though the thick hoar of dust which had accumulated on their shoes and garments from an obviously long journey lent a disadvantageous shabbiness to their appearance just now.

The man was of fine figure, swarthy, and stern in aspect; and he showed in profile a facial angle so slightly inclined as to be almost perpendicular. He wore a short jacket of brown corduroy, newer than the remainder of his suit, which was a fustian waistcoat with white horn buttons, breeches of the same, tanned leggings, and a straw hat overlaid with black glazed canvas. At his back he carried by a looped strap a rush basket, from which protruded at one end the crutch of a hay-knife, a wimble* for hay-bonds being also visible in the aperture. His measured, springless walk was the walk of the skilled countryman as distinct from the desultory shamble of the general labourer; while in the turn and plant of each foot there was, further, a dogged and cynical indifference personal to himself, showing its presence even in the regularly interchanging fustian folds, now in the left leg, now in the right, as he paced along.

What was really peculiar, however, in this couple's progress, and would have attracted the attention of any casual observer otherwise disposed to overlook them, was the perfect silence they preserved. They walked side by side in such a way as to suggest afar off the low, easy, confidential chat of people full of reciprocity; but on closer view it could be discerned that the man was reading, or pretending to read, a ballad sheet which he kept before his eyes with some difficulty by the hand that was passed through the basket strap.

That the man and woman were husband and wife, and the parents of the girl in arms, there could be little doubt. No other than such relationship would have accounted for the atmosphere of stale familiarity which the trio carried along with them like a nimbus as they moved down the road.

When the outlying houses of Weydon-Priors could just be descried,

---

* wimble: a kind of auger or gimlet

the family group was met by a turnip-hoer with his hoe on his shoulder, and his dinner-bag suspended from it. The reader promptly glanced up.

'Any trade doing here?' he asked phlegmatically, designating the village in his van by a wave of the broadsheet. And thinking the labourer did not understand him, he added, 'Anything in the hay-trussing line?'

The turnip-hoer had already begun shaking his head. 'Why, save the man, what wisdom's in him that 'a should come to Weydon for a job of that sort this time o' year?'

'Then is there any house to let – a little small new cottage just a builded, or such like?' asked the other.

The pessimist still maintained a negative. 'Pulling down is more the nater of Weydon. There were five houses cleared away last year, and three this; and the volk nowhere to go – no, not so much as a thatched hurdle; that's the way o' Weydon-Priors.'

The hay-trusser, which he obviously was, nodded with some superciliousness. Looking towards the village, he continued, 'There is something going on here, however, is there not?'

'Ay. 'Tis Fair Day. Though what you hear now is little more than the clatter and scurry of getting away the money o' children and fools, for the real business is done earlier than this. I've been working within sound o't all day, but I didn't go up – not I. 'Twas no business of mine.'

The trusser and his family proceeded on their way, and soon entered the Fair-field, which showed standing-places and pens where many hundreds of horses and sheep had been exhibited and sold in the forenoon, but were now in great part taken away. At present, as their informant had observed, but little real business remained on hand, the chief being the sale by auction of a few inferior animals, that could not otherwise be disposed of, and had been absolutely refused by the better class of traders, who came and went early. Yet the crowd was denser now than during the morning hours, the frivolous contingent of visitors, including journeymen* out for a holiday, a stray soldier or two come on furlough, village shopkeepers, and the like, having latterly flocked in; persons whose activities found a congenial field among the peep-shows, toy-stands, waxworks, inspired monsters, disinterested medical men who travelled for the public good, thimble-riggers,* nick-nack vendors, and readers of Fate.

Neither of our pedestrians had much heart for these things, and they looked around for a refreshment tent among the many which dotted the down. Two, which stood nearest to them in the ochreous haze of expiring sunlight, seemed almost equally inviting. One was formed of new, milk-hued canvas, and bore red flags on its summit; it announced 'Good

---

* journeymen: workmen who hire themselves out for the day (cf. French 'journée': day)

* thimble-riggers: cheats at a betting game called 'thimble and pea'

Home-brewed Beer, Ale, and Cyder.' The other was less new; a little iron stove-pipe came out of it at the back, and in front appeared the placard, 'Good Furmity Sold Hear.' The man mentally weighed the two inscriptions, and inclined to the former tent.

'No – no – the other one,' said the woman. 'I always like furmity; and so does Elizabeth-Jane; and so will you. It is nourishing after a long hard day.'

'I've never tasted it,' said the man. However, he gave way to her representations, and they entered the furmity booth forthwith.

A rather numerous company appeared within, seated at the long narrow tables that ran down the tent on each side. At the upper end stood a stove, containing a charcoal fire, over which hung a large three-legged crock, sufficiently polished round the rim to show that it was made of bell-metal. A haggish creature of about fifty presided, in a white apron, which, as it threw an air of respectability over her as far as it extended, was made so wide as to reach nearly round her waist. She slowly stirred the contents of the pot. The dull scrape of her large spoon was audible throughout the tent as she thus kept from burning the mixture of corn in the grain, flour, milk, raisins, currants, and what not, that composed the antiquated slop in which she dealt. Vessels holding the separate ingredients stood on a white-clothed table of boards and trestles close by.

The young man and woman ordered a basin each of the mixture, steaming hot, and sat down to consume it at leisure. This was very well so far, for furmity, as the woman had said, was nourishing, and as proper a food as could be obtained within the four seas; though, to those not accustomed to it, the grains of wheat swollen as large as lemon-pips, which floated on its surface, might have a deterrent effect at first.

But there was more in that tent than met the cursory glance; and the man, with the instinct of a perverse character, scented it quickly. After a mincing attack on his bowl, he watched the hag's proceedings from the corner of his eye, and saw the game she played. He winked to her, and passed up his basin in reply to her nod; when she took a bottle from under the table, slily measured out a quantity of its contents, and tipped the same into the man's furmity. The liquor poured in was rum. The man as slily sent back money in payment.

He found the concoction, thus strongly laced, much more to his satisfaction than it had been in its natural state. His wife had observed the proceeding with much uneasiness; but he persuaded her to have hers laced also, and she agreed to a milder allowance after some misgiving.

The man finished his basin, and called for another, the rum being signalled for in yet stronger proportion.

At the end of the first basin the man had risen to serenity; at the second he was jovial; at the third, argumentative; at the fourth, the qualities signified by the shape of his face, the occasional clench of his mouth, and the fiery spark of his dark eye, began to tell in his conduct; he was overbearing – even brilliantly quarrelsome.

The conversation took a high turn, as it often does on such occasions. The ruin of good men by bad wives, and, more particularly, the frustration of many a promising youth's high aims and hopes and the extinction of his energies by an early imprudent marriage, was the theme.

'I did for myself that way thoroughly,' said the trusser, with a contemplative bitterness that was well-nigh resentful. 'I married at eighteen, like the fool that I was; and this is the consequence o't.' He pointed at himself and family with a wave of the hand intended to bring out the penuriousness of the exhibition.

The young woman his wife, who seemed accustomed to such remarks, acted as if she did not hear them, and continued her intermittent private words on tender trifles to the sleeping and waking child, who was just big enough to be placed for a moment on the bench beside her when she wished to ease her arms. The man continued: –

'I haven't more than fifteen shillings in the world, and yet I am a good experienced hand in my line. I'd challenge England to beat me in the fodder business; and if I were a free man again I'd be worth a thousand pound before I'd done o't. But a fellow never knows these little things till all chance of acting upon 'em is past.'

The auctioneer selling the old horses in the field outside could be heard saying, 'Now this is the last lot – now who'll take the last lot for a song? Shall I say forty shillings? 'Tis a very promising brood-mare, a trifle over five years old, and nothing the matter with the hoss at all, except that she's a little holler in the back and had her left eye knocked out by the kick of another, her own sister, coming along the road.'

'For my part I don't see why men who have got wives and don't want 'em, shouldn't get rid of 'em as these gipsy fellows do their old horses,' said the man in the tent. 'Why shouldn't they put 'em up and sell 'em by auction to men who are in need of such articles? Hey? Why, begad, I'd sell mine this minute if anybody would buy her!'

'There's them that would do that,' some of the guests replied, looking at the woman, who was by no means ill-favoured.

'True,' said a smoking gentleman, whose coat had the fine polish about the collar, elbows, seams, and shoulder-blades that long-continued friction with grimy surfaces will produce, and which is usually more desired on furniture than on clothes. From his appearance he had possibly been in former time groom or coachman to some neighbouring county family. 'I've had my breedings in as good circles, I may say, as any man,' he added, 'and I know true cultivation, or nobody do; and I can declare she's got it – in the bone, mind ye, I say – as much as any female in the fair – though it may want a little bringing out.' Then, crossing his legs, he resumed his pipe with a nicely-adjusted gaze at a point in the air.

The fuddled young husband stared for a few seconds at this unexpected praise of his wife, half in doubt of the wisdom of his own attitude towards the possessor of such qualities. But he speedily lapsed into his former conviction, and said harshly: –

'Well, then, now is your chance; I am open to an offer for this gem o' creation.'

She turned to her husband and murmured, 'Michael, you have talked this nonsense in public places before. A joke is a joke, but you may make it once too often, mind!'

'I know I've said it before; I meant it. All I want is a buyer.'

The woman's manner changed, and her face assumed the grim shape and colour of which mention has been made.

'Mike, Mike,' said she; 'this is getting serious. Oh! – too serious!'

'Will anybody buy her?' said the man.

'I wish somebody would,' said she firmly. 'Her present owner is not at all to her liking!'

'Nor you to mine,' said he. 'So we are agreed about that. Gentlemen, you hear? It's an agreement to part. She shall take the girl if she wants to, and go her ways. I'll take my tools, and go my ways. 'Tis simple as Scripture history. Now then, stand up, Susan, and show yourself.'

'Don't, my chiel,' whispered a buxom staylace dealer in voluminous petticoats, who sat near the woman, 'yer good man don't know what he's saying.'

The woman, however, did stand up. 'Now, who's auctioneer?' cried the hay-trusser.

'I be,' promptly answered a short man, with a nose resembling a copper knob, a damp voice, and eyes like buttonholes. 'Who'll make an offer for this lady?'

The woman looked on the ground, as if she maintained her position by a supreme effort of will.

'Five shillings,' said some one, at which there was a laugh.

'No insults,' said the husband. 'Who'll say a guinea?'

Nobody answered; and the female dealer in staylaces interposed.

'Behave yerself moral, good man, for Heaven's love! Ah, what a cruelty is the poor soul married to! Bed and board is dear at some figures, 'pon my 'vation 'tis!'

'Set it higher, auctioneer,' said the trusser.

'Two guineas!' said the auctioneer; and no one replied.

'If they don't take her for that, in ten seconds they'll have to give more,' said the husband. 'Very well. Now, auctioneer, add another.'

'Three guineas – going for three guineas!' said the rheumy man.

'No bid?' said the husband. 'Good Lord, why she's cost me fifty times the money, if a penny. Go on.'

'Four guineas!' cried the auctioneer.

'I'll tell ye what – I won't sell her for less than five,' said the husband, bringing down his fist so that the basins danced. 'I'll sell her for five guineas to any man that will pay me the money, and treat her well; and he shall have her for ever, and never hear aught o' me. But she shan't go for less. Now then – five guineas – and she's yours. Susan, you agree?'

She bowed her head with absolute indifference.

'Five guineas,' said the auctioneer, 'or she'll be withdrawn. Do anybody give it? The last time. Yes or no?'

'Yes,' said a loud voice from the doorway.

All eyes were turned. Standing in the triangular opening which formed the door of the tent was a sailor, who, unobserved by the rest, had arrived there within the last two or three minutes. A dead silence followed his affirmation.

'You say you do?' asked the husband, staring at him.

'I say so,' replied the sailor.

'Saying is one thing, and paying is another. Where's the money?'

The sailor hesitated a moment, looked anew at the woman, came in, unfolded five crisp pieces of paper, and threw them down upon the table-cloth. They were Bank-of-England notes for five pounds. Upon the face of this he chinked down the shillings severally – one, two, three, four, five.

(Chapter 1)

The Mayor of Casterbridge

Almost twenty years on, Susan Newson, as she became after marrying the sailor, reappears in search of her first husband Michael Henchard. She arrives in Casterbridge with her daughter Elizabeth-Jane who, it is revealed later in Chapter 19, is not Henchard's own daughter.

A FEW score yards brought them to the spot where the town band was now shaking the window-panes with the strains of 'The Roast Beef of Old England.'

The building before whose doors they had pitched their music-stands was the chief hotel in Casterbridge – namely, the King's Arms. A spacious bow-window projected into the street over the main portico, and from the open sashes came the babble of voices, the jingle of glasses, and the drawing of corks. The blinds, moreover, being left unclosed, the whole interior of this room could be surveyed from the top of a flight of stone steps to the road-waggon office opposite, for which reason a knot of idlers had gathered there.

'We might, perhaps, after all, make a few inquiries about – our relation Mr. Henchard,' whispered Mrs. Newson who, since her entry into Casterbridge, had seemed strangely weak and agitated. 'And this, I think, would be a good place for trying it – just to ask, you know, how he stands in the town – if he is here, as I think he must be. You, Elizabeth-Jane, had better be the one to do it. I'm too worn out to do anything – pull down your fall* first.'

She sat down upon the lowest step, and Elizabeth-Jane obeyed her directions and stood among the idlers.

'What's going on to-night?' asked the girl, after singling out an old man and standing by him long enough to acquire a neighbourly right of converse.

'Well, ye must be a stranger sure,' said the old man, without taking his eyes from the window. 'Why, 'tis a great public dinner of the gentle-people and such like leading volk – wi' the Mayor in the chair. As we plainer fellows bain't invited, they leave the winder-shutters open that we may get jist a sense o't out here. If you mount the steps you can see 'em. That's Mr. Henchard, the Mayor, at the end of the table, a facing ye; and that's the Council men right and left. . . . Ah, lots of them when they begun life were no more than I be now!'

'Henchard!' said Elizabeth-Jane, surprised, but by no means suspecting the whole force of the revelation. She ascended to the top of the steps.

Her mother, though her head was bowed, had already caught from

---

* fall: veil

the inn-window tones that strangely riveted her attention, before the old man's words, 'Mr. Henchard, the Mayor,' reached her ears. She arose, and stepped up to her daughter's side as soon as she could do so without showing exceptional eagerness.

The interior of the hotel dining-room was spread out before her, with its tables, and glass, and plate, and inmates. Facing the window, in the chair of dignity, sat a man about forty years of age; of heavy frame, large features, and commanding voice; his general build being rather coarse than compact. He had a rich complexion, which verged on swarthiness, a flashing black eye, and dark, bushy brows and hair. When he indulged in an occasional loud laugh at some remark among the guests, his large mouth parted so far back as to show to the rays of the chandelier a full score or more of the two-and-thirty sound white teeth that he obviously still could boast of.

That laugh was not encouraging to strangers; and hence it may have been well that it was rarely heard. Many theories might have been built upon it. It fell in well with conjectures of a temperament which would have no pity for weakness, but would be ready to yield ungrudging admiration to greatness and strength. Its producer's personal goodness, if he had any, would be of a very fitful cast – an occasional almost oppressive generosity rather than a mild and constant kindness.

Susan Henchard's husband – in law, at least – sat before them, matured in shape, stiffened in line, exaggerated in traits; disciplined, thought-marked – in a word, older. Elizabeth, encumbered with no recollections as her mother was, regarded him with nothing more than the keen curiosity and interest which the discovery of such unexpected social standing in the long-sought relative naturally begot. He was dressed in an old-fashioned evening suit, an expanse of frilled shirt showing on his broad breast; jewelled studs, and a heavy gold chain. Three glasses stood at his right hand; but, to his wife's surprise, the two for wine were empty, while the third, a tumbler, was half full of water.

When last she had seen him he was sitting in a corduroy jacket, fustian waistcoat and breeches, and tanned leather leggings, with a basin of hot furmity before him. Time, the magician, had wrought much here. Watching him, and thus thinking of past days, she became so moved that she shrank back against the jamb of the waggon-office doorway to which the steps gave access, the shadow from it conveniently hiding her features. She forgot her daughter till a touch from Elizabeth-Jane aroused her. 'Have you seen him, mother?' whispered the girl.

'Yes, yes,' answered her companion hastily. 'I have seen him, and it is enough for me! Now I only want to go – pass away – die.'

'Why – Oh what?' She drew closer, and whispered in her mother's ear, 'Does he seem to you not likely to befriend us? I thought he looked a generous man. What a gentleman he is, isn't he? and how his diamond studs shine! How strange that you should have said he might be in the stocks, or in the workhouse, or dead! Did ever anything go more by contraries! Why do you feel so afraid of him? I am not at all; I'll call upon him – he can but say he don't own such remote kin.'

'I don't know at all – I can't tell what to set about. I feel so down.'

'Don't be that, mother, now we have got here and all! Rest there where you be a little while – I will look on and find out more about him.'

'I don't think I can ever meet Mr. Henchard. He is not how I thought he would be – he overpowers me! I don't wish to see him any more.'

'But wait a little time and consider.'

Elizabeth-Jane had never been so much interested in anything in her life as in their present position, partly from the natural elation she felt at discovering herself akin to a coach; and she gazed again at the scene. The younger guests were talking and eating with animation; their elders were searching for tit-bits, and sniffing and grunting over their plates like sows nuzzling for acorns. Three drinks seemed to be sacred to the company – port, sherry, and rum; outside which old-established trinity few or no palates ranged.

A row of ancient rummers* with ground figures on their sides, and each primed with a spoon, was now placed down the table, and these were promptly filled with grog at such high temperatures as to raise serious considerations for the articles exposed to its vapours. But Elizabeth-Jane noticed that, though this filling went on with great promptness up and down the table, nobody filled the Mayor's glass, who still drank large quantities of water from the tumbler behind the clump of crystal vessels intended for wine and spirits.

'They don't fill Mr. Henchard's wine-glasses,' she ventured to say to her elbow acquaintance, the old man.

'Ah, no; don't ye know him to be the celebrated abstaining worthy of that name? He scorns all tempting liquors; never touches nothing. Oh yes, he've strong qualities that way. I have heard tell that he sware a gospel oath in by-gone times, and has bode by it ever since. So they don't press him, knowing it would be unbecoming in the face of that; for yer gospel oath is a serious thing.'

Another elderly man, hearing this discourse, now joined in by inquiring, 'How much longer have he got to suffer from it, Solomon Longways?'

'Another two year, they say. I don't know the why and the wherefore of his fixing such a time, for 'a never has told anybody. But 'tis exactly two calendar years longer, they say. A powerful mind to hold out so long!'

---

* rummers: large drinking glasses

'True. . . . But there's great strength in hope. Knowing that in four-and-twenty months' time ye'll be out of your bondage, and able to make up for all you've suffered, by partaking without stint – why, it keeps a man up, no doubt.'

'No doubt, Christopher Coney, no doubt. And 'a must need such reflections – a lonely widow man,' said Longways.

'When did he lose his wife?' asked Elizabeth.

'I never knowed her. 'Twas afore he came to Casterbridge,' Solomon Longways replied with terminative emphasis, as if the fact of his ignorance of Mrs. Henchard were sufficient to deprive her history of all interest. 'But I know that 'a's a banded teetotaller, and that if any of his men be ever so little overtook by a drop he's down upon 'em as stern as the Lord upon the jovial Jews.'

'Has he many men, then?' said Elizabeth-Jane.

'Many! Why, my good maid, he's the powerfullest member of the Town Council, and quite a principal man in the country round besides. Never a big dealing in wheat, barley, oats, hay, roots, and such-like but Henchard's got a hand in it. Ay, and he'll go into other things too; and that's where he makes his mistake. He worked his way up from nothing when 'a came here; and now he's a pillar of the town. Not but what he's been shaken a little to-year about this bad corn he has supplied in his contracts. I've seen the sun rise over Durnover Moor these nine-and-sixty year, and though Mr. Henchard has never cussed me unfairly ever since I've worked for'n, seeing I be but a little small man, I must say that I have never before tasted such rough bread as has been made from Henchard's wheat lately. 'Tis that growed out that ye could a'most call it malt, and there's a list* at bottom o' the loaf as thick as the sole of one's shoe.'

The band now struck up another melody, and by the time it was ended the dinner was over, and speeches began to be made. The evening being calm, and the windows still open, these orations could be distinctly heard. Henchard's voice arose above the rest; he was telling a story of his hay-dealing experiences, in which he had outwitted a sharper who had been bent upon outwitting him.

'Ha-ha-ha!' responded his audience at the upshot of the story; and hilarity was general till a new voice arose with, 'This is all very well; but how about the bad bread?'

It came from the lower end of the table, where there sat a group of minor tradesmen who, although part of the company, appeared to be a little below the social level of the others; and who seemed to nourish a certain independence of opinion and carry on discussions not quite in

---

* list: inedible, unrisen dough

harmony with those at the head; just as the west end of a church is sometimes persistently found to sing out of time and tune with the leading spirits in the chancel.

This interruption about the bad bread afforded infinite satisfaction to the loungers outside, several of whom were in the mood which finds its pleasure in others' discomfiture; and hence they echoed pretty freely, 'Hey! How about the bad bread, Mr. Mayor?' Moreover, feeling none of the restraints of those who shared the feast, they could afford to add, 'You rather ought to tell the story o' that, sir!'

The interruption was sufficient to compel the Mayor to notice it.

'Well, I admit that the wheat turned out badly,' he said. 'But I was taken in in buying it as much as the bakers who bought it o' me.'

'And the poor folk who had to eat it whether or no,' said the inharmonious man outside the window.

Henchard's face darkened. There was temper under the thin bland surface – the temper which, artificially intensified, had banished a wife nearly a score of years before.

(Chapter 5)

The King's Arms, Casterbridge (see page 57).

In these intervening years Henchard had formed an intimate relationship with another woman, Lucetta Templeman. The reappearance of Susan coincides with the arrival of Lucetta, who has come to Casterbridge expecting to marry Henchard. It does not work out however, and she falls for the charms of the Scot, Donald Farfrae, and marries him.

But as always, the past will out. The locals, as so often in Hardy's stories, have been keeping themselves fully informed about the love lives of those above them in society. Here they are meeting in a Casterbridge inn of doubtful reputation, and plotting to reveal all about Henchard's past relationship with Lucetta.

THE INN called Peter's Finger was the church of Mixen Lane.
It was centrally situate, as such places should be, and bore about the same social relation to the Three Mariners as the latter bore to the King's Arms. At first sight the inn was so respectable as to be puzzling. The front door was kept shut, and the step was so clean that evidently but few persons entered over its sanded surface. But at the corner of the public-house was an alley, a mere slit, dividing it from the next building. Half-way up the alley was a narrow door, shiny and paintless from the rub of infinite hands and shoulders. This was the actual entrance to the inn.

The company at the Three Mariners were persons of quality in comparison with the company which gathered here; though it must be admitted that the lowest fringe of the Mariners' party touched the crest of Peter's at points. Waifs and strays of all sorts loitered about here. The landlady was a virtuous woman who years ago had been unjustly sent to gaol as an accessory to something or other after the fact. She underwent her twelvemonth, and had worn a martyr's countenance ever since, except at times of meeting the constable who apprehended her, when she winked her eye.

To this house Jopp* and his acquaintances had arrived. The settles on which they sat down were thin and tall, their tops being guyed by pieces of twine to hooks in the ceiling; for when the guests grew boisterous the settles would rock and overturn without some such security. The thunder of bowls echoed from the backyard; swingels* hung behind the blower of the chimney; and ex-poachers and ex-gamekeepers, whom squires had persecuted without a cause, sat elbowing each other – men who in past times had met in fights under the moon, till lapse of sentences on the one part, and loss of favour and expulsion from service on

* Jopp: a former employee of Henchard, who bears him a grudge (see chapter 26).

* swingels: cudgels

the other, brought them here together to a common level, where they sat calmly discussing old times.

'Dost mind how you could jerk a trout ashore with a bramble, and not ruffle the stream, Charl?' a deposed keeper was saying. ''Twas at that I caught 'ee once, if you can mind?'

'That can I. But the worst larry for me was that pheasant business at Yalbury Wood. Your wife swore false that time, Joe – Oh, by Gad, she did – there's no denying it.'

'How was that?' asked Jopp.

'Why – Joe closed wi' me, and we rolled down together, close to his garden hedge. Hearing the noise, out ran his wife with the oven pyle*, and it being dark under the trees she couldn't see which was uppermost. "Where beest thee, Joe, under or top?" she screeched. "Oh – under, by Gad!" says he. She then began to rap down upon my skull, back, and ribs with the pyle till we'd roll over again. "Where beest now, dear Joe, under or top?" she'd scream again. By George, 'twas through her I was took! And then when we got up in hall she sware that the cock pheasant was one of her rearing, when 'twas not your bird at all, Joe; 'twas Squire Brown's bird – that's whose 'twas – one that we'd picked off as we passed his wood, an hour afore. It did hurt my feelings to be so wronged! . . . Ah well – 'tis over now.'

'I might have had 'ee days afore that,' said the keeper. 'I was within a few yards of 'ee dozens of times, with a sight more of birds than that poor one.'

'Yes – 'tis not our greatest doings that the world gets wind of,' said the furmity-woman, who, lately settled in this purlieu, sat among the rest. Having travelled a great deal in her time she spoke with cosmopolitan largeness of idea. It was she who presently asked Jopp what was the parcel he kept so snugly under his arm.

'Ah, therein lies a grand secret,' said Jopp. 'It is the passion of love. To think that a woman should love one man so well, and hate another so unmercifully.'

'Who's the object of your meditation, sir?'

'One that stands high in this town. I'd like to shame her! Upon my life, 'twould be as good as a play to read her love-letters, the proud piece of silk and wax-work! For 'tis her love-letters that I've got here.'

'Love-letters? then let's hear 'em, good soul,' said Mother Cuxsom.* 'Lord, do ye mind, Richard, what fools we used to be when we were younger? Getting a schoolboy to write ours for us; and giving him a penny, do ye mind, not to tell other folks what he'd put inside, do ye mind?'

By this time Jopp had pushed his finger under the seals, and

---

* pyle: long handled shovel for putting loaves into ovens
* Mother Cuxsom, Nance Mockridge (see page 64) etc: local characters who first appear in Chapter 8.

unfastened the letters, tumbling them over and picking up one here and there at random, which he read aloud. These passages soon began to uncover the secret which Lucetta had so earnestly hoped to keep buried, though the epistles, being allusive only, did not make it altogether plain.

'Mrs. Farfrae wrote that!' said Nance Mockridge. ''Tis a humbling thing for us, as respectable women, that one of the same sex could do it. And now she's vowed herself to another man!'

'So much the better for her,' said the aged furmity-woman. 'Ah, I saved her from a real bad marriage, and she's never been the one to thank me.'

'I say, what a good foundation for a skimmity-ride*,' said Nance.

'True,' said Mrs. Cuxsom, reflecting. ''Tis as good a ground for a skimmity-ride as ever I knowed; and it ought not to be wasted. The last one seen in Casterbridge must have been ten years ago, if a day.'

At this moment there was a shrill whistle, and the landlady said to the man who had been called Charl, ''Tis Jim coming in. Would ye go and let down the bridge for me?'

Without replying Charl and his comrade Joe rose, and receiving a lantern from her went out at the back door and down the garden-path, which ended abruptly at the edge of the stream already mentioned. Beyond the stream was the open moor, from which a clammy breeze smote upon their faces as they advanced. Taking up the board that had lain in readiness one of them lowered it across the water, and the instant its further end touched the ground footsteps entered upon it, and there appeared from the shade a stalwart man with straps round his knees, a double-barrelled gun under his arm and some birds slung up behind him. They asked him if he had had much luck.

'Not much,' he said indifferently. 'All safe inside?'

Receiving a reply in the affirmative he went on inwards, the others withdrawing the bridge and beginning to retreat in his rear. Before, however, they had entered the house a cry of 'Ahoy' from the moor led them to pause.

The cry was repeated. They pushed the lantern into an outhouse, and went back to the brink of the stream.

'Ahoy – is this the way to Casterbridge?' said some one from the other side.

'Not in particular,' said Charl. 'There's a river afore 'ee.'

'I don't care – here's for through it!' said the man in the moor. 'I've had travelling enough for to-day.'

'Stop a minute, then,' said Charl, finding that the man was no enemy.

---

* skimmity-ride: skimmington ride. A practice universal under different names (e.g. in Warwickshire 'loo-belling', in some northern counties 'riding the stang'), throughout rural England. Those who were guilty, or were thought guilty of fornication or adultery were paraded in effigy to a fearful din. This was a relic of times when people involved were themselves made to 'ride the pole'.

Lucetta sees the skimmity-ride (see chapter 39). (Original illustration by Robert Barnes in The Graphic, *1 May 1886.)*

'Joe, bring the plank and lantern; here's somebody that's lost his way. You should have kept along the turnpike-road, friend, and not have strook across here.'

'I should – as I see now. But I saw a light here, and says I to myself, that's an outlying house, depend on't.'

The plank was now lowered; and the stranger's form shaped itself from the darkness. He was a middle-aged man, with hair and whiskers prematurely grey, and a broad and genial face. He had crossed on the plank without hesitation, and seemed to see nothing odd in the transit. He thanked them, and walked between them up the garden. 'What place is this?' he asked, when they reached the door.

'A public-house.'

'Ah. Perhaps it will suit me to put up at. Now then, come in and wet your whistle at my expense for the lift over you have given me.'

They followed him into the inn, where the increased light exhibited him as one who would stand higher in an estimate by the eye than in one by the ear. He was dressed with a certain clumsy richness – his coat being furred, and his head covered by a cap of seal-skin, which, though the nights were chilly, must have been warm for the daytime, spring being somewhat advanced. In his hand he carried a small mahogany case, strapped, and clamped with brass.

Apparently surprised at the kind of company which confronted him through the kitchen door, he at once abandoned his idea of putting up at the house; but taking the situation lightly, he called for glasses of the best, paid for them as he stood in the passage, and turned to proceed on his way by the front door. This was barred, and while the landlady was unfastening it the conversation about the skimmington was continued in the sitting-room, and reached his ears.

'What do they mean by a "skimmity-ride"?' he asked.

'O, sir!' said the landlady, swinging her long ear-rings with deprecating modesty; ''tis a' old foolish thing they do in these parts when a man's wife is – well, not too particularly his own. But as a respectable householder I don't encourage it.'

'Still, are they going to do it shortly? It is a good sight to see, I suppose?'

'Well, sir!' she simpered. And then, bursting into naturalness, and glancing from the corner of her eye, ''Tis the funniest thing under the sun! And it costs money.'

'Ah! I remember hearing of some such thing. Now I shall be in Casterbridge for two or three weeks to come, and should not mind seeing the performance. Wait a moment.' He turned back, entered the sitting-room, and said, 'Here, good folks; I should like to see the old custom you are talking of, and I don't mind being something towards it – take that.' He threw a sovereign on the table and returned to the landlady at the door, of whom, having inquired the way into the town, he took his leave.

(Chapter 36)

You can read the description of the skimmity ride in Chapter 39 and of its consequences in Chapter 40.

By the time of this extract, twenty-five years on, Henchard is a broken man both in business and in love. He knows that Elizabeth-Jane is not his daughter but Newson's, and that she is planning to marry the now widowed Farfrae. He has left Casterbridge to re-visit the place where he had sold his wife all those years ago.

The bright autumn sun shining into his eyes across the stubble awoke him the next morning early. He opened his basket and ate for his breakfast what he had packed for his supper; and in doing so overhauled the remainder of his kit. Although everything he brought necessitated carriage at his own back, he had secreted among his tools a few of Elizabeth-Jane's cast-off belongings, in the shape of gloves, shoes, a scrap of her handwriting, and the like; and in his pocket he carried a curl of her hair. Having looked at these things he closed them up again, and went onward.

During five consecutive days Henchard's rush basket rode along upon his shoulder between the highway hedges, the new yellow of the rushes catching the eye of an occasional field-labourer as he glanced through the quickset*, together with the wayfarer's hat and head, and down-turned face, over which the twig shadows moved in endless procession. It now became apparent that the direction of his journey was Weydon-Priors, which he reached on the afternoon of the sixth day.

The renowned hill whereon the annual fair had been held for so many generations was now bare of human beings, and almost of aught besides. A few sheep grazed thereabout, but these ran off when Henchard halted upon the summit. He deposited his basket upon the turf, and looked about with sad curiosity; till he discovered the road by which his wife and himself had entered on the upland so memorable to both, five-and-twenty years before.

'Yes, we came up that way,' he said, after ascertaining his bearings. 'She was carrying the baby, and I was reading a ballet-sheet. Then we crossed about here – she so sad and weary, and I speaking to her hardly at all, because of my cursed pride and mortification at being poor. Then we saw the tent – that must have stood more this way.' He walked to another spot; it was not really where the tent had stood, but it seemed so to him. 'Here we went in, and here we sat down. I faced this way. Then I drank, and committed my crime. It must have been just on that very pixy-ring that she was standing when she said her last words to me before going off with him; I can hear their sound now, and the sound of

---

* quickset: hedge

her sobs: "Oh Mike! I've lived with thee all this while, and had nothing but temper. Now I'm no more to 'ee – I'll try my luck elsewhere."'

He experienced not only the bitterness of a man who finds, in looking back upon an ambitious course, that what he has sacrificed in sentiment was worth as much as what he has gained in substance; but the super-added bitterness of seeing his very recantation nullified. He had been sorry for all this long ago; but his attempts to replace ambition by love had been as fully foiled as his ambition itself. His wronged wife had foiled them by a fraud so grandly simple as to be almost a virtue. It was an odd sequence that out of all this tampering with social law came that flower of Nature, Elizabeth. Part of his wish to wash his hands of life arose from his perception of its contrarious inconsistencies – of Nature's jaunty readiness to support unorthodox social principles.

He intended to go on from this place – visited as an act of penance – into another part of the country altogether. But he could not help thinking of Elizabeth, and the quarter of the horizon in which she lived. Out of this it happened that the centrifugal tendency imparted by weariness of the world was counteracted by the centripetal influence of his love for his stepdaughter. As a consequence, instead of following a straight course yet further away from Casterbridge, Henchard gradually, almost unconsciously, deflected from that right line of his first intention; till, by degrees, his wandering, like that of the Canadian woodsman, became part of a circle of which Casterbridge formed the centre. In ascending any particular hill he ascertained the bearings as nearly as he could by means of the sun, moon, or stars, and settled in his mind the exact direction in which Casterbridge and Elizabeth-Jane lay. Sneering at himself for his weakness he yet every hour – nay, every few minutes – conjectured her actions for the time being – her sitting down and rising up, her goings and comings, till thought of Newson's and Farfrae's counter-influence would pass like a cold blast over a pool, and efface her image. And then he would say of himself, 'Oh you fool! All this about a daughter who is no daughter of thine!'

At length he obtained employment at his own occupation of hay-trusser, work of that sort being in demand at this autumn time. The scene of his hiring was a pastoral farm near the old western highway, whose course was the channel of all such communications as passed between the busy centres of novelty and the remote Wessex boroughs. He had chosen the neighbourhood of this artery from a sense that, situated here, though at a distance of fifty miles, he was virtually nearer to her whose welfare was so dear than he would be at a roadless spot only half as remote.

And thus Henchard found himself again on the precise standing which he had occupied a quarter of a century before.

He often kept an eager ear upon the conversation of those who passed along the road – not from a general curiosity by any means – but in the hope that among these travellers between Casterbridge and London some would, sooner or later, speak of the former place. The distance, however, was too great to lend much probability to his desire; and the highest result of his attention to wayside words was that he did indeed hear the name 'Casterbridge' uttered one day by the driver of a road-waggon. Henchard ran to the gate of the field he worked in, and hailed the speaker, who was a stranger.

'Yes – I've come from there, maister,' he said, in answer to Henchard's inquiry. 'I trade up and down, ye know; though, what with this travelling without horses that's getting so common, my work will soon be done.'

'Anything moving in the old place, mid I ask?'

'All the same as usual.'

'I've heard that Mr. Farfrae, the late mayor, is thinking of getting married. Now is that true or not?'

'I couldn't say for the life o' me. Oh no, I should think not.'

'But yes, John – you forget,' said a woman inside the waggon-tilt. 'What were them packages we carr'd there at the beginning o' the week? Surely they said a wedding was coming off soon – on Martin's Day*?'

The man declared he remembered nothing about it; and the waggon went on jangling over the hill.

Henchard was convinced that the woman's memory served her well. The date was an extremely probable one, there being no reason for delay on either side. He might, for that matter, write and inquire of Elizabeth; but his instinct for sequestration had made the course difficult. Yet before he left her she had said that for him to be absent from her wedding was not as she wished it to be.

(Chapter 44)

---

* Martin's Day: Martinmas – 11th November

Henchard does return, taking with him a wedding present of a caged goldfinch. He eventually dies a lonely man in absolute poverty, leaving his own epitaph pinned above his bed.

MICHAEL HENCHARD'S WILL

'That Elizabeth-Jane Farfrae be not told of my death, or made to grieve on account of me.
'& that I be not bury'd in consecrated ground.
'& that no sexton be asked to toll the bell.
'& that nobody is wished to see my dead body.
'& that no murners walk behind me at my funeral.
'& that no flours be planted on my grave.
'& that no man remember me.
'To this I put my name.

'MICHAEL HENCHARD.'

Rose-Ann

Why didn't you say you was promised, Rose-Ann?
   Why didn't you name it to me,
Ere ever you tempted me hither, Rose-Ann,
   So often, so wearifully?

O why did you let me be near 'ee, Rose-Ann,
   Talking things about wedlock so free,
And never by nod or by whisper, Rose-Ann,
   Give a hint that it wasn't to be?

Down home I was raising a flock of stock ewes,
   Cocks and hens, and wee chickens by scores,
And lavendered linen all ready to use,
   A-dreaming that they would be yours.

Mother said: 'She's a sport-making maiden, my son;'
   And a pretty sharp quarrel had we;
O why do you prove by this wrong you have done
   That I saw not what mother could see?

Never once did you say you was promised, Rose-Ann,
   Never once did I dream it to be;
And it cuts to the heart to be treated, Rose-Ann,
   As you in your scorning treat me!

The Wedding Morning

Tabitha dressed for her wedding: –
   'Tabby, why look so sad?'
'– O I feel a great gloominess spreading, spreading,
   Instead of supremely glad! . . .

'I called on Carry last night,
   And he came whilst I was there,
Not knowing I'd called. So I kept out of sight,
   And I heard what he said to her:

' " – Ah, I'd far liefer marry
   You, Dear, to-morrow!" he said,
"But that cannot be." – O I'd give him to Carry,
   And willingly see them wed,

'But how can I do it when
   His baby will soon be born?
After that I hope I may die. And then
   She can have him. I shall not mourn!'

Julie-Jane

SING; how 'a would sing!
How 'a would raise the tune
When we rode in the waggon from harvesting
    By the light o' the moon!

Dance; how 'a would dance!
If a fiddlestring did but sound
She would hold out her coats,* give a slanting glance,
    And go round and round.

Laugh; how 'a would laugh!
Her peony lips would part
As if none such a place for a lover to quaff
    At the deeps of a heart.

Julie, O girl of joy,
  Soon, soon that lover he came,
Ah, yes: and gave thee a baby-boy,
    But never his name. . . .

– Tolling for her, as you guess;
  And the baby too. . . . 'Tis well,
You knew her in maidhood likewise? – Yes,
    That's her burial bell.

'I suppose,' with a laugh, she said,
'I should blush that I'm not a wife;
But how can it matter, so soon to be dead.
    What one does in life!'

When we sat making the mourning
  By her death-bed side, said she,
'Dears, how can you keep from your lovers, adorning
    In honour of me!'

Bubbling and brightsome eyed!
  But now – O never again.
She chose her bearers before she died
    From her fancy-men.

* coats: old name for petticoats.

Note. It is, or was, a common custom in Wessex, and probably other country places, to prepare the mourning beside the death-bed, the dying person sometimes assisting, even selecting the bearers for the funeral.

Tess of the D'Urbervilles

Tess Durbeyfield: beloved and betrayed

Tess of the D'Urbervilles was first printed in serial form in **The Graphic** from 4 July to 26 December 1891.

> 'After reading the book, it is Tess who fills one's mind and haunts one's imagination, and in the heart-rending pity of her story, one is little able to pause and do justice to the bits of rustic chorus, the wonderful description of Wessex scenery in the changes of the seasons, never better done by Mr. Hardy than in this book. . . .

> 'We acknowledge that Mr. Hardy is not one of our first favourites in fiction, and that this new book [**Tess**] is not greatly to our taste. Taste, as everybody knows, is the one thing upon which there is no discussion. Some of us. . . sincerely like the literature that suits the young person, and some prefer to have their novels hot, and lock them up in cupboards for their private delectation. Though we strongly object to being instructed in any illegitimate way, yet, for our own part, we prefer cleanly lives, and honest sentiment, and a novel which is round and contains everything, not 'the relations between the sexes' alone.'
> (Mrs. Oliphant, **Blackwood's Magazine**, March 1892)

John Durbeyfield, a small local carrier, learns that he is a descendant of the ancient family of the D'Urbervilles, still wealthy landowners in the district. The revelation turns his head and is the basic cause of the misfortunes that dog his luckless daughter, Tess.

Her seduction by Alex D'Urberville wrecks her marriage to Angel Clare, who refuses to live with her when she tells him her story, and goes abroad.

Alex comes back into her life, persuades her that her husband will never return and she joins him for the sake of the help it will bring to her needy family.

But Angel Clare does come back. . . . .

Believing that they might be descended from a wealthy landowning family, Joan and John Durbeyfield send their eldest daughter, Tess, to the d'Urberville mansion, in the hope of making a worthwhile connection.

Every day seemed to throw upon her young shoulders more of the family burdens, and that Tess should be the representative of the Durbeyfields at the d'Urberville mansion came as a thing of course. In this instance it must be admitted that the Durbeyfields were putting their fairest side outward.

She alighted from the van at Trantridge Cross, and ascended on foot a hill in the direction of the district known as The Chase, on the borders of which, as she had been informed, Mrs. d'Urberville's seat, The Slopes, would be found. It was not a manorial home in the ordinary sense, with fields, and pastures, and a grumbling farmer, out of whom the owner had to squeeze an income for himself and his family by hook or by crook. It was more, far more; a country-house built for enjoyment pure and simple, with not an acre of troublesome land attached to it beyond what was required for residential purposes, and for a little fancy farm kept in hand by the owner, and tended by a bailiff.

The crimson brick lodge came first in sight, up to its eaves in dense evergreens. Tess thought this was the mansion itself till, passing through the side wicket with some trepidation, and onward to a point at which the drive took a turn, the house proper stood in full view. It was of recent erection – indeed almost new – and of the same rich red colour that formed such a contrast with the evergreens of the lodge. Far behind the corner of the house – which rose like a geranium bloom against the subdued colours around – stretched the soft azure landscape of The Chase – a truly venerable tract of forest land, one of the few remaining woodlands in England of undoubted primaeval date, wherein Druidical mistletoe was still found on aged oaks, and where enormous yew-trees, not planted by the hand of man, grew as they had grown when they were pollarded for bows. All this sylvan antiquity, however, though visible from The Slopes, was outside the immediate boundaries of the estate.

Everything on this snug property was bright, thriving, and well kept; acres of glass-houses stretched down the inclines to the copses at their feet. Everything looked like money – like the last coin issued from the Mint. The stables, partly screened by Austrian pines and evergreen oaks, and fitted with every late appliance, were as dignified as Chapels-of-Ease.* On the extensive lawn stood an ornamental tent, its door being towards her.

---

* Chapels-of-Ease: chapels for those who live a long way from their parish church

Simple Tess Durbeyfield stood at gaze, in a half-alarmed attitude, on the edge of the gravel sweep. Her feet had brought her onward to this point before she had quite realized where she was; and now all was contrary to her expectation.

'I thought we were an old family; but this is all new!' she said, in her artlessness. She wished that she had not fallen in so readily with her mother's plans for 'claiming kin,' and had endeavoured to gain assistance nearer home.

The d'Urbervilles – or Stoke-d'Urbervilles, as they at first called themselves – who owned all this, were a somewhat unusual family to find in such an old-fashioned part of the country. Parson Tringham had spoken truly when he said that our shambling John Durbeyfield was the only really lineal representative of the old d'Urberville family existing in the county, or near it; he might have added, what he knew very well, that the Stoke-d'Urbervilles were no more d'Urbervilles of the true tree than he was himself. Yet it must be admitted that this family formed a very good stock whereon to regraft a name which sadly wanted such renovation.

When old Mr. Simon Stoke, latterly deceased, had made his fortune as an honest merchant (some said money-lender) in the North, he decided to settle as a county man in the South of England, out of hail of his business district; and in doing this he felt the necessity of recommencing with a name that would not too readily identify him with the smart tradesman of the past, and that would be less commonplace than the original bald stark words. Conning for an hour in the British Museum the pages of works devoted to extinct, half-extinct, obscured, and ruined families appertaining to the quarter of England in which he proposed to settle, he considered that *d'Urberville* looked and sounded as well as any of them: and d'Urberville accordingly was annexed to his own name for himself and his heirs eternally. Yet he was not an extravagant-minded man in this, and in constructing his family tree on the new basis was duly reasonable in framing his inter-marriages and aristocratic links, never inserting a single title above a rank of strict moderation.

Of this work of imagination poor Tess and her parents were naturally in ignorance – much to their discomfiture; indeed, the very possibility of such annexations was unknown to them; who supposed that, though to be well-favoured might be the gift of fortune, a family name came by nature.

Tess still stood hesitating like a bather about to make his plunge, hardly knowing whether to retreat or to persevere, when a figure came forth from the dark triangular door of the tent. It was that of a tall young man, smoking.

He had an almost swarthy complexion, with full lips, badly moulded, though red and smooth, above which was a well-groomed black moustache with curled points, though his age could not be more than three- or four-and-twenty. Despite the touches of barbarism in his contours, there was a singular force in the gentleman's face, and in his bold rolling eye.

'Well, my Beauty, what can I do for you?' said he, coming forward. And perceiving that she stood quite confounded: 'Never mind me. I am Mr. d'Urberville. Have you come to see me or my mother?'

This embodiment of a d'Urberville and a namesake differed even more from what Tess had expected than the house and grounds had differed. She had dreamed of an aged and dignified face, the sublimation of all the d'Urberville lineaments, furrowed with incarnate memories representing in hieroglyphic the centuries of her family's and England's history. But she screwed herself up to the work in hand, since she could not get out of it, and answered: –

'I came to see your mother, sir.'

'I am afraid you cannot see her – she is an invalid,' replied the present representative of the spurious house; for this was Mr. Alec, the only son of the lately deceased gentleman. 'Cannot I answer your purpose? What is the business you wish to see her about?'

'It isn't business – it is – I can hardly say what!'

'Pleasure?'

'Oh no. Why, sir, if I tell you, it will seem—'

Tess's sense of a certain ludicrousness in her errand was now so strong that, notwithstanding her awe of him, and her general discomfort at being here, her rosy lips curved towards a smile, much to the attraction of the swarthy Alexander.

'It is so very foolish,' she stammered; 'I fear I can't tell you!'

'Never mind; I like foolish things. Try again, my dear,' said he kindly.

'Mother asked me to come,' Tess continued; 'and, indeed, I was in the mind to do so myself likewise. But I did not think it would be like this. I came, sir, to tell you that we are of the same family as you.'

'Ho! Poor relations?'

'Yes.'

'Stokes?'

'No; d'Urbervilles.'

'Ay, ay; I mean d'Urbervilles.'

'Our names are worn away to Durbeyfield; but we have several proofs that we are d'Urbervilles. Antiquarians hold we are, – and – and we have an old seal, marked with a ramping lion on a shield, and a castle over him. And we have a very old silver spoon, round in the bowl like a little ladle, and marked with the same castle. But it is so worn that mother uses it to stir the pea-soup.'

'A castle argent is certainly my crest,' said he blandly. 'And my arms a lion rampant.'

'And so mother said we ought to make ourselves beknown to you – as we've lost our horse by a bad accident, and are the oldest branch o' the family.'

'Very kind of your mother, I'm sure. And I, for one, don't regret her step.' Alec looked at Tess as he spoke, in a way that made her blush a little. 'And so, my pretty girl, you've come on a friendly visit to us, as relations?'

'I suppose I have,' faltered Tess, looking uncomfortable again.

'Well – there's no harm in it. Where do you live? What are you?'

She gave him brief particulars; and responding to further inquiries told him that she was intending to go back by the same carrier who had brought her.

'It is a long while before he returns past Trantridge Cross. Supposing we walk round the grounds to pass the time, my pretty coz?'

Tess wished to abridge her visit as much as possible; but the young man was pressing, and she consented to accompany him. He conducted her about the lawns, and flower-beds, and conservatories; and thence to the fruit-garden and greenhouses, where he asked her if she liked strawberries.

'Yes,' said Tess, 'when they come.'

'They are already here.' D'Urberville began gathering specimens of the fruit for her, handing them back to her as he stooped; and, presently, selecting a specially fine product of the 'British Queen' variety, he stood up and held it by the stem to her mouth.

'No – no!' she said quickly, putting her fingers between his hand and her lips. 'I would rather take it in my own hand.'

'Nonsense!' he insisted; and in a slight distress she parted her lips and took it in.

They had spent some time wandering desultorily thus, Tess eating in a half-pleased, half-reluctant state whatever d'Urberville offered her. When she could consume no more of the strawberries he filled her little basket with them; and then the two passed round to the rose trees, whence he gathered blossoms and gave her to put in her bosom. She obeyed like one in a dream, and when she could affix no more he himself tucked a bud or two into her hat, and heaped her basket with others in the prodigality of his bounty. At last, looking at his watch, he said, 'Now, by the time you have had something to eat, it will be time for you to leave, if you want to catch the carrier to Shaston. Come here, and I'll see what grub I can find.'

Stoke-d'Urberville took her back to the lawn and into the tent, where he left her, soon reappearing with a basket of light luncheon, which he put before her himself. It was evidently the gentleman's wish not to be disturbed in this pleasant *tête-à-tête* by the servantry.

'Do you mind my smoking?' he asked.

'Oh, not at all, sir.'

He watched her pretty and unconscious munching through the skeins of smoke that pervaded the tent, and Tess Durbeyfield did not divine, as she innocently looked down at the roses in her bosom, that there behind the blue narcotic haze was potentially the 'tragic mischief' of her drama – one who stood fair to be the blood-red ray in the spectrum of her young life. She had an attribute which amounted to a disadvantage just now; and it was this that caused Alec d'Urberville's eyes to rivet themselves upon her. It was a luxuriance of aspect, a fulness of growth, which made her appear more of a woman than she really was. She had inherited the feature from her mother without the quality it denoted. It had troubled her mind occasionally, till her companions had said that it was a fault which time would cure.

She soon had finished her lunch. 'Now I am going home, sir,' she said, rising.

'And what do they call you?' he asked, as he accompanied her along the drive till they were out of sight of the house.

'Tess Durbeyfield, down at Marlott.'

'And you say your people have lost their horse?'

'I – killed him!' she answered, her eyes filling with tears as she gave particulars of Prince's death. 'And I don't know what to do for father on account of it!'

'I must think if I cannot do something. My mother must find a berth for you. But, Tess, no nonsense about "d'Urberville"; – "Durbeyfield" only, you know – quite another name.'

'I wish for no better, sir,' said she with something of dignity.

For a moment – only for a moment – when they were in the turning of the drive, between the tall rhododendrons and conifers, before the lodge became visible, he inclined his face towards her as if – but, no: he thought better of it, and let her go.

Thus the thing began. Had she perceived this meeting's import she might have asked why she was doomed to be seen and coveted that day by the wrong man, and not by some other man, the right and desired one in all respects – as nearly as humanity can supply the right and desired; yet to him who amongst her acquaintance might have approximated to this kind, she was but a transient impression, half forgotten.

In the ill-judged execution of the well-judged plan of things the call seldom produces the comer, the man to love rarely coincides with the hour for loving. Nature does not often say 'See!' to her poor creature at a time when seeing can lead to happy doing; or reply 'Here!' to a body's cry of 'Where?' till the hide-and-seek has become an irksome, outworn game. We may wonder whether at the acme and summit of the human progress these anachronisms will be corrected by a finer intuition, a closer interaction of the social machinery than that which now jolts us round and along; but such completeness is not to be prophesied, or even conceived as possible. Enough that in the present case, as in millions, it was not the two halves of a perfect whole that confronted each other at the perfect moment; a missing counterpart wandered independently about the earth waiting in crass obtuseness till the late time came. Out of which maladroit delay sprang anxieties, disappointments, shocks, catastrophes, and passing-strange destinies.

When d'Urberville got back to the tent he sat down astride on a chair reflecting, with a pleased gleam in his face. Then he broke into a loud laugh.

'Well, I'm damned! What a funny thing! Ha-ha-ha! And what a crumby* girl!'

(Chapter 5)

---

* crumby: appetising; luscious (slang)

This first encounter with Alec d'Urberville leads to Tess taking up a position in the household to care for the ageing Mrs. d'Urberville.

Her next significant meeting with Alec is one upon which the rest of the story hinges. It occurs when he has offered to ride her home on his horse after she had been to a local fair.

THE TWAIN cantered along for some time without speech, Tess as she clung to him still panting in her triumph, yet in other respects dubious. She had perceived that the horse was not the spirited one he sometimes rode, and felt no alarm on that score, though her seat was precarious enough despite her tight hold of him. She begged him to slow the animal to a walk, which Alec accordingly did.

'Neatly done, was it not, dear Tess?' he said by and by.

'Yes!' said she. 'I am sure I ought to be much obliged to you.'

'And are you?'

She did not reply.

'Tess, why do you always dislike my kissing you?'

'I suppose—because I don't love you.'

'You are quite sure?'

'I am angry with you sometimes!'

'Ah, I half feared as much.' Nevertheless, Alec did not object to that confession. He knew that anything was better than frigidity. 'Why haven't you told me when I have made you angry?'

'You know very well why. Because I cannot help myself here.'

'I haven't offended you often by love-making?'

'You have sometimes.'

'How many times?'

'You know as well as I – too many times.'

'Every time I have tried?'

She was silent, and the horse ambled along for a considerable distance, till a faint luminous fog, which had hung in the hollows all the evening, became general and enveloped them. It seemed to hold the moonlight in suspension, rendering it more pervasive than in clear air. Whether on this account, or from absent-mindedness, or from sleepiness, she did not perceive that they had long ago passed the point at which the lane to Trantridge branched from the highway, and that her conductor had not taken the Trantridge track.

She was inexpressibly weary. She had risen at five o'clock every morning of that week, had been on foot the whole of each day, and on this evening had in addition walked the three miles to Chaseborough, waited three hours for her neighbours without eating or drinking, her impatience to start them preventing either; she had then walked a mile of the way home, and had undergone the excitement of the quarrel, till, with the slow progress of their steed, it was now nearly one o'clock. Only once, however, was she overcome by actual drowsiness. In that moment of oblivion her head sank gently against him.

D'Urberville stopped the horse, withdrew his feet from the stirrups, turned sideways on the saddle, and enclosed her waist with his arm to support her.

This immediately put her on the defensive, and with one of those sudden impulses of reprisal to which she was liable she gave him a little push from her. In his ticklish position he nearly lost his balance and only just avoided rolling over into the road, the horse, though a powerful one, being fortunately the quietest he rode.

'That is devilish unkind!' he said. 'I mean no harm – only to keep you from falling.'

She pondered suspiciously; till, thinking that this might after all be true, she relented, and said quite humbly, 'I beg your pardon, sir.'

'I won't pardon you unless you show some confidence in me. Good God!' he burst out, 'what am I, to be repulsed so by a mere chit like you? For near three mortal months have you trifled with my feelings, eluded me, and snubbed me; and I won't stand it!'

'I'll leave you to-morrow, sir.'

'No, you will not leave me to-morrow! Will you, I ask once more, show your belief in me by letting me clasp you with my arm? Come, between us two and nobody else, now. We know each other well; and you know that I love you, and think you the prettiest girl in the world, which you are. Mayn't I treat you as a lover?'

She drew a quick pettish breath of objection, writhing uneasily on her seat, looked far ahead, and murmured, 'I don't know – I wish – how can I say yes or no when—'

He settled the matter by clasping his arm round her as he desired, and Tess expressed no further negative. Thus they sidled slowly onward till it struck her they had been advancing for an unconscionable time – far longer than was usually occupied by the short journey from Chaseborough, even at this walking pace, and that they were no longer on hard road, but in a mere trackway.

'Why, where be we?' she exclaimed.

'Passing by a wood.'

'A wood – what wood? Surely we are quite out of the road?'

'A bit of The Chase – the oldest wood in England. It is a lovely night, and why should we not prolong our ride a little?'

'How could you be so treacherous!' said Tess, between archness and real dismay, and getting rid of his arm by pulling open his fingers one by one, though at the risk of slipping off herself. 'Just when I've been putting such trust in you, and obliging you to please you, because I thought I had wronged you by that push! Please set me down, and let me walk home.'

'You cannot walk home, darling, even if the air were clear. We are miles away from Trantridge, if I must tell you, and in this growing fog you might wander for hours among these trees.'

'Never mind that,' she coaxed. 'Put me down, I beg you. I don't mind where it is; only let me get down, sir, please!'

'Very well, then, I will – on one condition. Having brought you here to this out-of-the-way place, I feel myself responsible for your safe-conduct home, whatever you may yourself feel about it. As to your getting to Trantridge without assistance, it is quite impossible; for, to tell the truth, dear, owing to this fog, which so disguises everything, I don't quite know where we are myself. Now, if you will promise to wait beside the horse while I walk through the bushes till I come to some road or house, and ascertain exactly our whereabouts, I'll deposit you here willingly. When I come back I'll give you full directions, and if you insist upon walking you may; or you may ride – at your pleasure.'

She accepted these terms, and slid off on the near side, though not till he had stolen a cursory kiss. He sprang down on the other side.

'I suppose I must hold the horse?' said she.

'Oh no; it's not necessary,' replied Alec, patting the panting creature. 'He's had enough of it for to-night.'

He turned the horse's head into the bushes, hitched him on to a bough, and made a sort of couch or nest for her in the deep mass of dead leaves.

'Now, you sit there,' he said. 'The leaves have not got damp as yet. Just give an eye to the horse – it will be quite sufficient.'

He took a few steps away from her, but, returning, said, 'By the bye, Tess, your father has a new cob to-day. Somebody gave it to him.'

'Somebody? You!'

D'Urberville nodded.

'Oh how very good of you that is!' she exclaimed, with a painful sense of the awkwardness of having to thank him just then.

'And the children have some toys.'

'I didn't know – you ever sent them anything!' she murmured, much moved. 'I almost wish you had not – yes, I almost wish it!'

'Why, dear?'

'It – hampers me so.'

'Tessy – don't you love me ever so little now?'

'I'm grateful,' she reluctantly admitted. 'But I fear I do not—' The sudden vision of his passion for herself as a factor in this result so distressed her that, beginning with one slow tear, and then following with another, she wept outright.

'Don't cry, dear, dear one! Now sit down here, and wait till I come.' She passively sat down amid the leaves he had heaped, and shivered slightly. 'Are you cold?' he asked.

'Not very – a little.'

He touched her with his fingers, which sank into her as into down. 'You have only that puffy muslin dress on – how's that?'

'It's my best summer one. 'Twas very warm when I started, and I didn't know I was going to ride, and that it would be night.'

'Nights grow chilly in September. Let me see.' He pulled off a light overcoat that he had worn, and put it round her tenderly. 'That's it – now you'll feel warmer,' he continued. 'Now, my pretty, rest there; I shall soon be back again.'

Having buttoned the overcoat round her shoulders he plunged into the webs of vapour which by this time formed veils between the trees. She could hear the rustling of the branches as he ascended the adjoining slope, till his movements were no louder than the hopping of a bird, and finally died away. With the setting of the moon the pale light lessened, and Tess became invisible as she fell into reverie upon the leaves where he had left her.

In the meantime Alec d'Urberville had pushed on up the slope to clear his genuine doubt as to the quarter of The Chase they were in. He had, in fact, ridden quite at random for over an hour, taking any turning that came to hand in order to prolong companionship with her, and giving far more attention to Tess's moonlit person than to any wayside object. A little rest for the jaded animal being desirable, he did not hasten his search for landmarks. A clamber over the hill into the adjoining vale brought him to the fence of a highway whose contours he recognized, which settled the question of their whereabouts. D'Urberville thereupon turned back; but by this time the moon had quite gone down, and partly on account of the fog The Chase was wrapped in thick darkness, although morning was not far off. He was obliged to advance with outstretched hands to avoid contact with the boughs, and discovered that to hit the exact spot from which he had started was at first entirely beyond him. Roaming up and down, round and round, he at length heard a slight movement of the horse close at hand; and the sleeve of his overcoat unexpectedly caught his foot.

'Tess!' said d'Urberville.

There was no answer. The obscurity was now so great that he could see absolutely nothing but a pale nebulousness at his feet, which represented the white muslin figure he had left upon the dead leaves. Everything else was blackness alike. D'Urberville stooped; and heard a gentle regular breathing. He knelt and bent lower, till her breath warmed his face, and in a moment his cheek was in contact with hers. She was sleeping soundly, and upon her eyelashes there lingered tears.

Darkness and silence ruled everywhere around. Above them rose the primaeval yews and oaks of The Chase, in which there poised gentle roosting birds in their last nap; and about them stole the hopping rabbits and hares. But, might some say, where was Tess's guardian angel? where was the providence of her simple faith?

Why it was that upon this beautiful feminine tissue, sensitive as gossamer, and practically blank as snow as yet, there should have been traced such a coarse pattern as it was doomed to receive; why so often the coarse appropriates the finer thus, the wrong man the woman, the wrong woman the man, many thousand years of analytical philosophy have failed to explain to our sense of order. One may, indeed, admit the possibility of a retribution lurking in the present catastrophe. Doubtless some of Tess d'Urberville's mailed ancestors rollicking home from a fray had dealt the same measure even more ruthlessly towards peasant girls of their time. But though to visit the sins of the fathers upon the children may be a morality good enough for divinities, it is scorned by average human nature; and it therefore does not mend the matter.

As Tess's own people down in those retreats are never tired of saying among each other in their fatalistic way: 'It was to be.' There lay the pity of it. An immeasurable social chasm was to divide our heroine's personality thereafter from that previous self of hers who stepped from her mother's door to try her fortune at Trantridge poultry-farm.

(Chapter 11)

Tess becomes pregnant. She returns to her family home but her illegitimate baby son survives for only a few weeks. She leaves to start a new life as a dairymaid on a farm many miles from her home. It is while she is working here that she falls in love with the man she will eventually marry – Angel Clare. The following episode includes one of their early encounters.

THE HOT weather of July had crept upon them unawares, and the atmosphere of the flat vale hung heavy as an opiate over the dairy-folk, the cows, and the trees. Hot steaming rains fell frequently, making the grass where the cows fed yet more rank, and hindering the late haymaking in the other meads.

It was Sunday morning; the milking was done; the outdoor milkers had gone home. Tess and the other three were dressing themselves rapidly, the whole bevy having agreed to go together to Mellstock Church, which lay some three or four miles distant from the dairy-house. She had now been two months at Talbothays, and this was her first excursion.

All the preceding afternoon and night heavy thunderstorms had hissed down upon the meads, and washed some of the hay into the river; but this morning the sun shone out all the more brilliantly for the deluge, and the air was balmy and clear.

The crooked lane leading from their own parish to Mellstock ran along the lowest levels in a portion of its length, and when the girls reached the most depressed spot they found that the result of the rain had been to flood the lane over-shoe to a distance of some fifty yards. This would have been no serious hindrance on a week-day; they would have clicked through it in their high pattens and boots quite unconcerned; but on this day of vanity, this Sun's-day, when flesh went forth to coquet with flesh while hypocritically affecting business with spiritual things; on this occasion for wearing their white stockings and thin shoes, and their pink, white, and lilac gowns, on which every mud spot would be visible, the pool was an awkward impediment. They could hear the church-bell calling – as yet nearly a mile off.

'Who would have expected such a rise in the river in summer-time!' said Marian, from the top of the roadside bank on which they had climbed, and were maintaining a precarious footing in the hope of creeping along its slope till they were past the pool.

'We can't get there anyhow, without walking right through it, or else going round the Turnpike way; and that would make us so very late!' said Retty, pausing hopelessly.

'And I do colour up so hot, walking into church late, and all the people staring round,' said Marian, 'that I hardly cool down again till we get into the That-it-may-please-Thees.'

While they stood clinging to the bank they heard a splashing round the bend of the road, and presently appeared Angel Clare, advancing along the lane towards them through the water.

Four hearts gave a big throb simultaneously.

His aspect was probably as un-Sabbatarian a one as a dogmatic parson's son often presented; his attire being his dairy clothes, long wading boots, a cabbage-leaf inside his hat to keep his head cool, with a thistle-spud* to finish him off.

'He's not going to church,' said Marian.

'No – I wish he was!' murmured Tess.

Angel, in fact, rightly or wrongly (to adopt the safe phrase of evasive controversialists), preferred sermons in stones to sermons in churches and chapels on fine summer days. This morning, moreover, he had gone out to see if the damage to the hay by the flood was considerable or not. On his walk he observed the girls from a long distance, though they had been so occupied with their difficulties of passage as not to notice him. He knew that the water had risen at that spot, and that it would quite check their progress. So he had hastened on, with a dim idea of how he could help them – one of them in particular.

The rosy-cheeked, bright-eyed quartet looked so charming in their light summer attire, clinging to the roadside bank like pigeons on a roof-slope, that he stopped a moment to regard them before coming close. Their gauzy skirts had brushed up from the grass innumerable flies and butterflies which, unable to escape, remained caged in the transparent tissue as in an aviary. Angel's eye at last fell upon Tess, the hindmost of the four; she, being full of suppressed laughter at their dilemma, could not help meeting his glance radiantly.

He came beneath them in the water, which did not rise over his long boots; and stood looking at the entrapped flies and butterflies.

'Are you trying to get to church?' he said to Marian, who was in front, including the next two in his remark, but avoiding Tess.

'Yes, sir; and 'tis getting late; and my colour do come up so—'

'I'll carry you through the pool – every Jill of you.'

The whole four flushed as if one heart beat through them.

'I think you can't, sir,' said Marian.

'It is the only way for you to get past. Stand still. Nonsense – you are not too heavy! I'd carry you all four together. Now, Marian, attend,' he continued, 'and put your arms round my shoulders, so. Now! Hold on. That's well done.'

---

* thistle spud: a tool for weeding out thistles

Marian had lowered herself upon his arm and shoulder as directed, and Angel strode off with her, his slim figure, as viewed from behind, looking like the mere stem to the great nosegay suggested by hers. They disappeared round the curve of the road, and only his sousing footsteps and the top ribbon of Marian's bonnet told where they were. In a few minutes he reappeared. Izz Huett was the next in order upon the bank.

'Here he comes,' she murmured, and they could hear that her lips were dry with emotion. 'And I have to put my arms round his neck and look into his face as Marian did.'

'There's nothing in that,' said Tess quickly.

'There's a time for everything,' continued Izz, unheeding. 'A time to embrace, and a time to refrain from embracing; the first is now going to be mine.'

'Fie – it is Scripture*, Izz!'

'Yes,' said Izz, 'I've always a' ear at church for pretty verses.'

Angel Clare, to whom three-quarters of this performance was a commonplace act of kindness, now approached Izz. She quietly and dreamily lowered herself into his arms, and Angel methodically marched off with her. When he was heard returning for the third time Retty's throbbing heart could be almost seen to shake her. He went up to the redhaired girl, and while he was seizing her he glanced at Tess. His lips could not have pronounced more plainly, 'It will soon be you and I.' Her comprehension appeared in her face; she could not help it. There was an understanding between them.

Poor little Retty, though by far the lightest weight, was the most troublesome of Clare's burdens. Marian had been like a sack of meal, a dead weight of plumpness under which he had literally staggered. Izz had ridden sensibly and calmly. Retty was a bunch of hysterics.

However, he got through with the disquieted creature, deposited her, and returned. Tess could see over the hedge the distant three in a group, standing as he had placed them on the next rising ground. It was now her turn. She was embarrassed to discover that excitement at the proximity of Mr. Clare's breath and eyes, which she had condemned in her companions, was intensified in herself; and as if fearful of betraying her secret she paltered with him at the last moment.

'I may be able to clim' along the bank perhaps – I can clim' better than they. You must be so tired, Mr. Clare!'

'No, no, Tess,' said he quickly. And almost before she was aware she was seated in his arms and resting against his shoulder.

'Three Leahs* to get one Rachel,' he whispered.

'They are better women than I,' she replied, magnanimously sticking to her resolve.

---

* Scripture: a biblical reference to *Ecclesiastes 3:5*, 'to everything there is a season.. a time to embrace', etc.

* Leah: a biblical reference to *Genesis 29*. Jacob is deceived into marrying Leah before he eventually marries Rachel.

'Not to me,' said Angel.

He saw her grow warm at this; and they went some steps in silence.

'I hope I am not too heavy?' she said timidly.

'Oh no. You should lift Marian! Such a lump. You are like an undulating billow warmed by the sun. And all this fluff of muslin about you is the froth.'

'It is very pretty – if I seem like that to you.'

'Do you know that I have undergone three-quarters of this labour entirely for the sake of the fourth quarter?'

'No.'

'I did not expect such an event to-day.'

'Nor I. . . . The water came up so sudden.'

That the rise in the water was what she understood him to refer to, the state of her breathing belied. Clare stood still and inclined his face towards hers.

'Oh Tessy!' he exclaimed.

The girl's cheeks burned to the breeze, and she could not look into his eyes for her emotion. It reminded Angel that he was somewhat unfairly taking advantage of an accidental position; and he went no further with it. No definite words of love had crossed their lips as yet, and suspension at this point was desirable now. However, he walked slowly, to make the remainder of the distance as long as possible; but at last they came to the bend, and the rest of their progress was in full view of the other three. The dry land was reached, and he set her down.

Her friends were looking with round thoughtful eyes at her and him, and she could see that they had been talking of her. He hastily bade them farewell, and splashed back along the stretch of submerged road.

The four moved on together as before, till Marian broke the silence by saying: –

'No – in all truth; we have no chance against her!' She looked joylessly at Tess.

'What do you mean?' asked the latter.

'He likes 'ee best – the very best! We could see it as he brought 'ee. He would have kissed 'ee, if you had encouraged him to do it, ever so little.'

'No, no,' said she.

(Chapter 23)

It is hard to imagine how this episode could have offended public taste, but it did. When the story first appeared, in serial form, the publishers insisted that Clare should transport the dairymaids through the water in a wheelbarrow!

Tess with Angel Clare. (Original illustration by E. Borough Johnson in The Graphic, *22 August 1891.)*

It is equally hard to believe how Clare behaves after they are married, when Tess confides in him about her past with Alec d'Urberville. He had confessed to her about an occasion when he 'plunged into eight-and-forty hours' dissipation with a stranger', but when he has heard Tess's story he is less than Christian in his reaction.

CLARE performed the irrelevant act of stirring the fire; the intelligence had not even yet got to the bottom of him. After stirring the embers he rose to his feet; all the force of her disclosure had imparted itself now. His face had withered. In the strenuousness of his concentration he treadled fitfully on the floor. He could not, by any contrivance, think closely enough; that was the meaning of his vague movement. When he spoke it was in the most inadequate, commonplace voice of the many varied tones she had heard from him.

'Tess!'

'Yes, dearest.'

'Am I to believe this? From your manner I am to take it as true. Oh you cannot be out of your mind! You ought to be! Yet you are not. . . . My wife, my Tess – nothing in you warrants such a supposition as that?'

'I am not out of my mind,' she said.

'And yet—' He looked vacantly at her, to resume with dazed senses: 'Why didn't you tell me before? Ah, yes, you would have told me, in a way – but I hindered you, I remember!'

These and other of his words were nothing but the perfunctory babble of the surface while the depths remained paralyzed. He turned away, and bent over a chair. Tess followed him to the middle of the room where he was, and stood there staring at him with eyes that did not weep. Presently she slid down upon her knees beside his foot, and from this position she crouched in a heap.

'In the name of our love, forgive me!' she whispered with a dry mouth. 'I have forgiven you for the same!'

And, as he did not answer, she said again: –

'Forgive me as you are forgiven! *I* forgive *you*, Angel.'

'You – yes, you do.'

'But you do not forgive me?'

'Oh Tess, forgiveness does not apply to the case! You were one person; now you are another. My God – how can forgiveness meet such a grotesque – prestidigitation as that!'

He paused, contemplating this definition; then suddenly broke into horrible laughter – as unnatural and ghastly as a laugh in hell.

'Don't – don't! It kills me quite, that!' she shrieked. 'Oh have mercy upon me – have mercy!'

He did not answer; and, sickly white, she jumped up.

'Angel, Angel! what do you mean by that laugh?' she cried out. 'Do you know what this is to me?'

He shook his head.

'I have been hoping, longing, praying, to make you happy! I have thought what joy it will be to do it, what an unworthy wife I shall be if I do not! That's what I have felt, Angel!'

'I know that.'

'I thought, Angel, that you loved me – me, my very self! If it is I you do love, Oh how can it be that you look and speak so? It frightens me! Having begun to love you, I love you for ever – in all changes, in all disgraces, because you are yourself. I ask no more. Then how can you, Oh my own husband, stop loving me?'

'I repeat, the woman I have been loving is not you.'

'But who?'

'Another woman in your shape.'

She perceived in his words the realization of her own apprehensive foreboding in former times. He looked upon her as a species of impostor; a guilty woman in the guise of an innocent one. Terror was upon her white face as she saw it; her cheek was flaccid, and her mouth had almost the aspect of a round little hole. The horrible sense of his view of her so deadened her that she staggered; and he stepped forward, thinking she was going to fall.

'Sit down, sit down,' he said gently. 'You are ill; and it is natural that you should be.'

She did sit down, without knowing where she was, that strained look still upon her face, and her eyes such as to make his flesh creep.

'I don't belong to you any more, then; do I, Angel?' she asked helplessly. 'It is not me, but another woman like me that he loved, he says.'

The image raised caused her to take pity upon herself as one who was ill-used. Her eyes filled as she regarded her position further; she turned round and burst into a flood of self-sympathetic tears.

Clare was relieved at this change, for the effect on her of what had happened was beginning to be a trouble to him only less than the woe of the disclosure itself. He waited patiently, apathetically, till the violence of her grief had worn itself out, and her rush of weeping had lessened to a catching gasp at intervals.

'Angel,' she said suddenly, in her natural tones, the insane, dry voice of terror having left her now. 'Angel, am I too wicked for you and me to live together?'

'I have not been able to think what we can do.'

'I shan't ask you to let me live with you, Angel, because I have no right to! I shall not write to mother and sisters to say we be married, as I said I would do; and I shan't finish the good-hussif* I cut out and meant to make while we were in lodgings.'

'Shan't you?'

'No, I shan't do anything, unless you order me to; and if you go away from me I shall not follow 'ee; and if you never speak to me any more I shall not ask why, unless you tell me I may.'

'And if I order you to do anything?'

'I will obey you like your wretched slave, even if it is to lie down and die.'

'You are very good. But it strikes me that there is a want of harmony between your present mood of self-sacrifice and your past mood of self-preservation.'

These were the first words of antagonism. To fling elaborate sarcasms at Tess, however, was much like flinging them at a dog or cat. The charms of their subtlety passed by her unappreciated, and she only received them as inimical sounds which meant that anger ruled. She remained mute, not knowing that he was smothering his affection for her. She hardly observed that a tear descended slowly upon his cheek, a tear so large that it magnified the pores of the skin over which it rolled, like the object lens of a microscope. Meanwhile reillumination as to the terrible and total change that her confession had wrought in his life, in his universe, returned to him, and he tried desperately to advance among the new conditions in which he stood. Some consequent action was necessary; yet what?

'Tess,' he said, as gently as he could speak, 'I cannot stay – in this room – just now. I will walk out a little way.'

He quietly left the room, and the two glasses of wine that he had poured out for their supper – one for her, one for him – remained on the table untasted.

The closing of the door behind him, gently as it had been pulled to, roused Tess from her stupor. He was gone; she could not stay. Hastily flinging her cloak around her she opened the door and followed, putting out the candles as if she were never coming back. The rain was over and the night was now clear.

She was soon close at his heels, for Clare walked slowly and without purpose. His form beside her light gray figure looked black, sinister, and forbidding, and she felt as sarcasm the touch of the jewels of which she had been momentarily so proud. Clare turned at hearing her footsteps, but his recognition of her presence seemed to make no difference to him,

---

* good-hussif: a bag to contain needlework items

and he went on over the five yawning arches of the great bridge in front of the house.

The cow and horse tracks in the road were full of water, the rain having been enough to charge them, but not enough to wash them away. Across these minute pools the reflected stars flitted in a quick transit as she passed; she would not have known they were shining overhead if she had not seen them there – the vastest things of the universe imaged in objects so mean.

The place to which they had travelled to-day was in the same valley as Talbothays, but some miles lower down the river; and the surroundings being open she kept easily in sight of him. Away from the house the road wound through the meads, and along these she followed Clare without any attempt to come up with him or to attract him, but with dumb and vacant fidelity.

At last, however, her listless walk brought her up alongside him, and still he said nothing.

'What have I done – what *have* I done! I have not told of anything that interferes with or belies my love for you. You don't think I planned it, do you? It is in your own mind what you are angry at, Angel; it is not in me. Oh, it is not in me, and I am not that deceitful woman you think me!'

'H'm – well. Not deceitful, my wife; but not the same. No, not the same. But do not make me reproach you. I have sworn that I will not; and I will do everything to avoid it.'

But she went on pleading in her distraction; and perhaps said things that would have been better left to silence.

'Angel! – Angel! I was a child – a child when it happened! I knew nothing of men.'

'You were more sinned against than sinning, that I admit.'

'Then will you not forgive me?'

'I do forgive you, but forgiveness is not all.'

'And love me?'

To this question he did not answer.

(Chapter 35)

Clare decides he cannot continue to live with Tess and goes off to South America to pursue his farming career.

Alec comes back into her life, persuading her that her husband will never return. She joins him for the sake of the help it will bring to her needy family.

But, after almost two years, Angel Clare does come back and traces Tess to Sandbourne where she is living with Alec d'Urberville.

At eleven o'clock that night, having secured a bed at one of the hotels and telegraphed his address to his father immediately on his arrival, he walked out into the streets of Sandbourne. It was too late to call on or inquire for any one, and he reluctantly postponed his purpose till the morning. But he could not retire to rest just yet.

This fashionable watering-place, with its eastern and its western stations, its piers, its groves of pines, its promenades, and its covered gardens, was, to Angel Clare, like a fairy place suddenly created by the stroke of a wand, and allowed to get a little dusty. An outlying eastern tract of the enormous Egdon Waste was close at hand, yet on the very verge of that tawny piece of antiquity such a glittering novelty as this pleasure city had chosen to spring up. Within the space of a mile from its outskirts every irregularity of the soil was prehistoric, every channel an undisturbed British trackway; not a sod having been turned there since the days of the Cæsars. Yet the exotic had grown here, suddenly as the prophet's gourd*; and had drawn hither Tess.

By the midnight lamps he went up and down the winding way of this new world in an old one, and could discern between the trees and against the stars the lofty roofs, chimneys, gazebos, and towers of the numerous fanciful residences of which the place was composed. It was a city of detached mansions; a Mediterranean lounging-place on the English Channel; and as seen now by night it seemed even more imposing than it was.

The sea was near at hand, but not intrusive; it murmured, and he thought it was the pines; the pines murmured in precisely the same tones, and he thought they were the sea.

Where could Tess possibly be, a cottage-girl, his young wife, amidst all this wealth and fashion? The more he pondered the more was he puzzled. Were there any cows to milk here? There certainly were no fields to till. She was most probably engaged to do something in one of these large houses; and he sauntered along, looking at the chamber-windows and their lights going out one by one; and wondered which of them might be hers.

Conjecture was useless, and just after twelve o'clock he entered and went to bed. Before putting out his light he re-read Tess's impassioned

---

* prophet's gourd: a biblical reference to *Jonah 4: 5–10*. God makes a gourd come up overnight to protect Jonah from the sun.

letter. Sleep, however, he could not, – so near her, yet so far from her – and he continually lifted the window-blind and regarded the backs of the opposite houses, and wondered behind which of the sashes she reposed at that moment.

He might almost as well have sat up all night. In the morning he arose at seven, and shortly after went out, taking the direction of the chief post-office. At the door he met an intelligent postman coming out with letters for the morning delivery.

'Do you know the address of a Mrs. Clare?' asked Angel.

The postman shook his head.

Then, remembering that she would have been likely to continue the use of her maiden name, Clare said: –

'Or a Miss Durbeyfield?'

'Durbeyfield?'

This also was strange to the postman addressed.

'There's visitors coming and going every day, as you know, sir,' he said; 'and without the name of the house 'tis impossible to find 'em.'

One of his comrades hastening out at that moment, the name was repeated to him.

'I know no name of Durbeyfield; but there is the name of d'Urberville at The Herons,' said the second.

'That's it!' cried Clare, pleased to think that she had reverted to the real pronunciation. 'What place is The Herons?'

'A stylish lodging-house. 'Tis all lodging-houses here, bless 'ee.'

Clare received directions how to find the house, and hastened thither, arriving with the milkman. The Herons, though an ordinary villa, stood in its own grounds, and was certainly the last place in which one would have expected to find lodgings, so private was its appearance. If poor Tess was a servant here, as he feared, she would go to the back-door to that milkman, and he was inclined to go thither also. However, in his doubts he turned to the front, and rang.

The hour being early the landlady herself opened the door. Clare inquired for Teresa d'Urberville or Durbeyfield.

'Mrs. d'Urberville?'

'Yes.'

Tess, then, passed as a married woman, and he felt glad, even though she had not adopted his name.

'Will you kindly tell her that a relative is anxious to see her?'

'It is rather early. What name shall I give, sir?'

'Angel.'

'Mr. Angel?'

'No; Angel. It is my Christian name. She'll understand.'

'I'll see if she is awake.'

He was shown into the front room – the dining-room – and looked out through the spring curtains at the little lawn, and the rhododendrons and other shrubs upon it. Obviously her position was by no means so bad as he had feared, and it crossed his mind that she must somehow have claimed and sold the jewels to attain it. He did not blame her for one moment. Soon his sharpened ear detected footsteps upon the stairs, at which his heart thumped so painfully that he could hardly stand firm. 'Dear me! what will she think of me, so altered as I am!' he said to himself; and the door opened.

Tess appeared on the threshold – not at all as he had expected to see her – bewilderingly otherwise, indeed. Her great natural beauty was, if not heightened, rendered more obvious by her attire. She was loosely wrapped in a cashmere dressing-gown of gray-white, embroidered in half-mourning tints, and she wore slippers of the same hue. Her neck rose out of a frill of down, and her well-remembered cable of dark-brown hair was partially coiled up in a mass at the back of her head and partly hanging on her shoulder – the evident result of haste.

He had held out his arms, but they had fallen again to his side; for she had not come forward, remaining still in the opening of the doorway. Mere yellow skeleton that he was now he felt the contrast between them, and thought his appearance distasteful to her.

'Tess!' he said huskily, 'can you forgive me for going away? Can't you – come to me? How do you get to be – like this?'

'It is too late,' said she, her voice sounding hard through the room, her eyes shining unnaturally.

'I did not think rightly of you – I did not see you as you were!' he continued to plead. 'I have learnt to since, dearest Tessy mine!'

'Too late, too late!' she said, waving her hand in the impatience of a person whose tortures cause every instant to seem an hour. 'Don't come close to me, Angel! No – you must not. Keep away.'

'But don't you love me, my dear wife, because I have been so pulled down by illness? You are not so fickle – I am come on purpose for you – my mother and father will welcome you now!'

'Yes – Oh, yes, yes! But I say, I say it is too late.'

She seemed to feel like a fugitive in a dream, who tries to move away, but cannot. 'Don't you know all – don't you know it? Yet how do you come here if you do not know?'

'I inquired here and there, and I found the way.'

'I waited and waited for you,' she went on, her tones suddenly resuming their old fluty pathos. 'But you did not come! And I wrote to you, and you did not come! He kept on saying you would never come any more, and that I was a foolish woman. He was very kind to me, and to mother, and to all of us after father's death. He—'

'I don't understand.'

'He has won me back to him.'

Clare looked at her keenly, then, gathering her meaning, flagged like one plague-stricken, and his glance sank; it fell on her hands, which, once rosy, were now white and more delicate.

She continued: –

'He is upstairs. I hate him now, because he told me a lie – that you would not come again; and you *have* come! These clothes are what he's put upon me: I didn't care what he did wi' me! But – will you go away, Angel, please, and never come any more?'

They stood fixed, their baffled hearts looking out of their eyes with a joylessness pitiful to see. Both seemed to implore something to shelter them from reality.

'Ah – it is my fault!' said Clare.

But he could not get on. Speech was as inexpressive as silence. But he had a vague consciousness of one thing, though it was not clear to him till later; that his original Tess had spiritually ceased to recognize the body before him as hers – allowing it to drift, like a corpse upon the current, in a direction dissociated from its living will.

A few instants passed, and he found that Tess was gone. His face grew colder and more shrunken as he stood concentrated on the moment, and a minute or two after he found himself in the street, walking along he did not know whither.

(Chapter 55)

These extracts have illustrated the seduction, the love and the betrayal.
Read the last four chapters for the murder!

Tess and Angel Clare at Stonehenge (see chapter 58). (Original illustration by Daniel A. Wehrschmidt in The Graphic, *26 December 1891.)*

The Ruined Maid

'O'MELIA, my dear, this does everything crown!
   Who could have supposed I should meet you in Town?
And whence such fair garments, such prosperi-ty?' –
'O didn't you know I'd been ruined?' said she.

– 'You left us in tatters, without shoes or socks,
Tired of digging potatoes, and spudding up docks;
And now you've gay bracelets and bright feathers three!' –
'Yes: that's how we dress when we're ruined,' said she.

– 'At home in the barton you said "thee" and "thou",
And "thik oon", and "theäs oon", and "t'other"; but now
Your talking quite fits 'ee for high compa-ny!' –
'Some polish is gained with one's ruin,' said she.

– 'Your hands were like paws then, your face blue and bleak
But now I'm bewitched by your delicate cheek,
And your little gloves fit as on any la-dy!' –
'We never do work when we're ruined,' said she.

– 'You used to call home-life a hag-ridden dream,
And you'd sigh, and you'd sock; but at present you seem
To know not of megrims or melancho-ly!' –
'True. One's pretty lively when ruined,' said she.

– 'I wish I had feathers, a fine sweeping gown,
And a delicate face, and could strut about Town!' –
'My dear – a raw country girl, such as you be,
Cannot quite expect that. You ain't ruined,' said she.

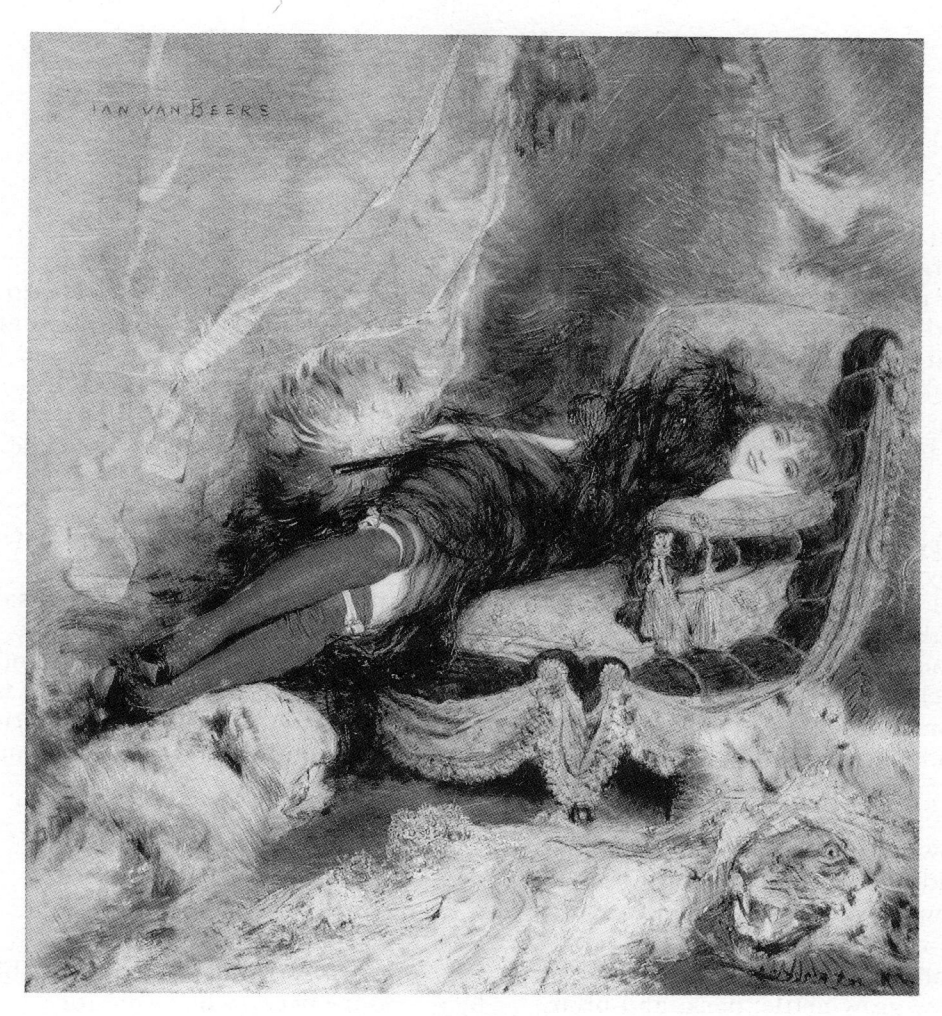

The Courtesan by Jan Van Beers.
'"Some polish is gained with one's ruin," said she.'

Tess's Lament

I

I would that folk forgot me quite,
    Forgot me quite!
I would that I could shrink from sight,
    And no more see the sun.
Would it were time to say farewell,
To claim my nook, to need my knell,
Time for them all to stand and tell
    Of my day's work as done.

II

Ah! dairy where I lived so long,
    I lived so long;
Where I would rise up staunch and strong,
    And lie down hopefully.
Twas there within the chimney-seat
He watched me to the clock's slow beat –
Loved me, and learnt to call me Sweet,
    And whispered words to me.

III

And now he's gone; and now he's gone;...
    And now he's gone!
The flowers we potted perhaps are thrown
    To rot upon the farm.
And where we had our supper-fire
May now grow nettle, dock, and briar,
And all the place be mould and mire
    So cozy once and warm.

IV

And it was I who did it all,
    Who did it all;
T'was I who made the blow to fall
    On him who thought no guile.
Well, it is finished – past, and he
Has left me to my misery
And I must take my cross on me
    For wronging him a while.

V

How gay we looked that day we wed,
    That day we wed!
May joy be with ye! they all said
    A-standing by the durn.*
I wonder what they say o'us now,
And if they know my lot; and how
She feels who milks my favourite cow,
    And takes my place at churn!

VI

It wears me out to think of it,
    To think of it;
I cannot bear my fate as writ,
    I'd have my life unbe;
Would turn my memory to a blot,
Make every relic of me rot,
My doings be as they were not,
    And gone all trace of me!

---

* durn: (dialect) a door-post

Note: It is probable that Hardy wrote this poem during the time when he made a dramatization of *Tess of the D'Urbervilles*, in 1894–5.

Short Stories:
A Few Crusted Characters

'These vans, so numerous hereabout, are a respectable, if somewhat lumbering, class of conveyance, much resorted to by decent travellers. . . .' (Introduction: A Few Crusted Characters)

Two crusted Dorset characters

A Few Crusted Characters

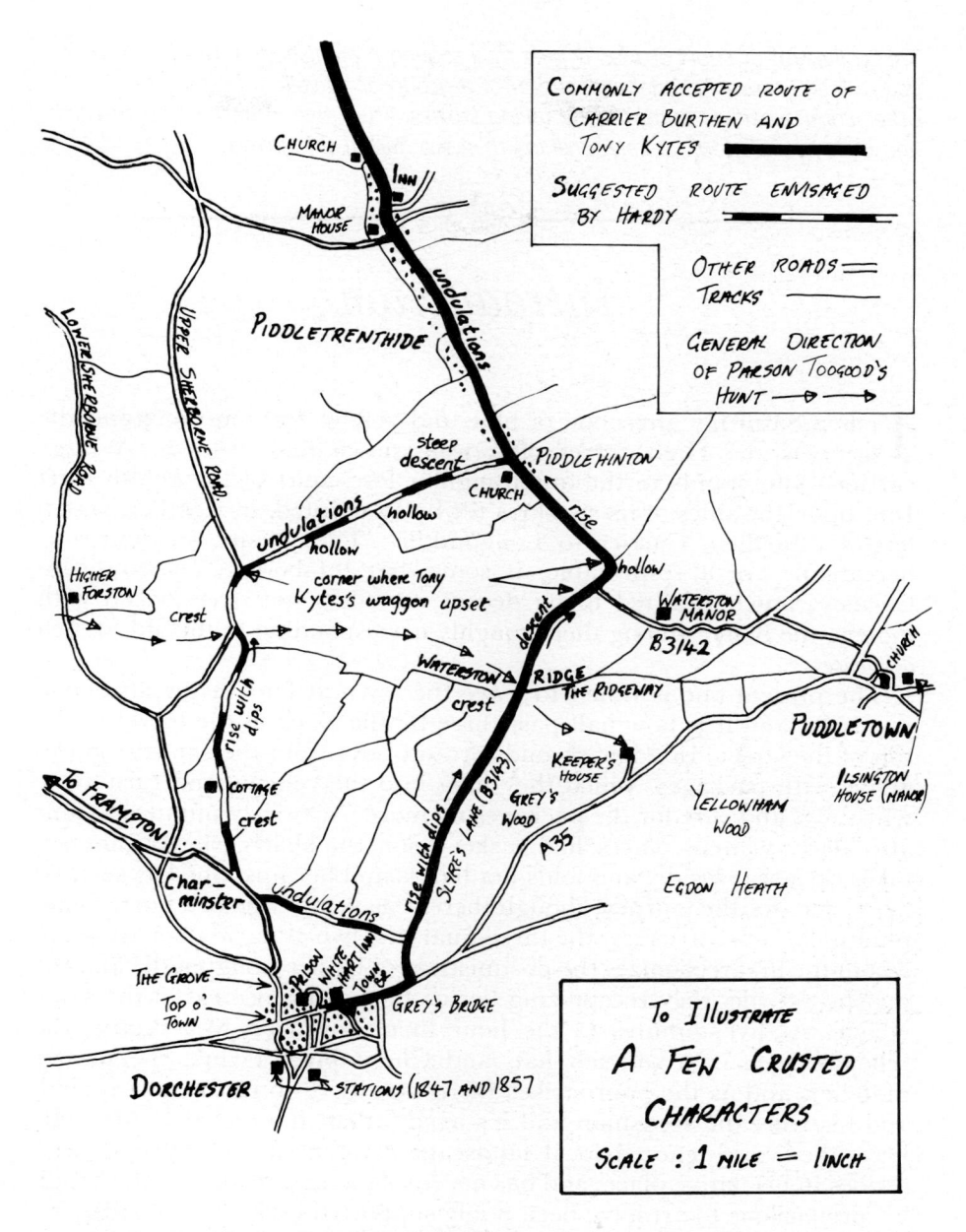

Local historians and students of Hardy often derive great satisfaction from relating the fictional settings to the actual places, in this case the area between Dorchester and the Piddle Valley, north of Puddletown.

A Few Crusted Characters

This collection of short stories is part of a sequence published in 1891. Hardy uses a well known fictional convention of a group of travellers keeping each other entertained on a journey by telling stories. They give a more down-to-earth and light-hearted look at relationships than we find in the novels.

Introduction

It is a Saturday afternoon of blue and yellow autumn-time, and the scene is the High Street of a well-known market-town. A large carrier's van stands in the quadrangular fore-court of the White Hart Inn, upon the sides of its spacious tilt being painted, in weather-beaten letters: 'Burthen, Carrier to Longpuddle'. These vans, so numerous hereabout, are a respectable, if somewhat lumbering, class of conveyance, much resorted to by decent travellers not overstocked with money, the better among them roughly corresponding to the old French *diligences*.

The present one is timed to leave the town at four in the afternoon precisely, and it is now half-past three by the clock in the turret at the top of the street. In a few seconds errand-boys from the shops begin to arrive with packages, which they fling into the vehicle, and turn away whistling, and care for the packages no more. At twenty minutes to four an elderly woman places her basket upon the shafts, slowly mounts, takes up a seat inside, and folds her hands and her lips. She has secured her corner for the journey, though there is as yet no sign of a horse being put in, nor of a carrier. At the three-quarters, two other women arrive, in whom the first recognizes the postmistress of Upper Longpuddle and the registrar's wife, they recognizing her as the aged groceress of the same village. At five minutes to the hour there approach Mr. Profitt, the schoolmaster, in a soft felt hat, and Christopher Twink, the master thatcher; and as the hour strikes there rapidly drop in the parish clerk and his wife, the seedsman and his aged father, the registrar; also Mr. Day, the world-ignored local landscape-painter, an elderly man who resides in his native place, and has never sold a picture outside it, though his pretensions to art have been nobly supported by his fellow villagers, whose confidence in his genius has been as remarkable as the outer neglect of it, leading them to buy his paintings so extensively (at the price of a few shillings each, it is true) that every dwelling in the parish exhibits three or four of those admired productions on its walls.

Burthen, the carrier, is by this time seen bustling round the vehicle; the horses are put in, the proprietor arranges the reins and springs up into his seat as if he were used to it – which he is.

'Is everybody here?' he asks preparatorily over his shoulder to the passengers within.

As those who were not there did not reply in the negative the muster was assumed to be complete, and after a few hitches and hindrances the van with its human freight was got under way. It jogged on at an easy pace till it reached the bridge which formed the last outpost of the town. The carrier pulled up suddenly.

'Bless my soul!' he said, 'I've forgot the curate!'

All who could do so gazed from the little back-window of the van, but the curate was not in sight.

'Now I wonder where that there man is?' continued the carrier.

'Poor man, he ought to have a living at his time of life.'

'And he ought to be punctual,' said the carrier. ' "Four o'clock sharp is my time for starting," I said to 'en. And he said, "I'll be there." Now he's not here; and as a serious old church-minister he ought to be as good as his word. Perhaps Mr. Flaxton knows, being in the same line of life?' He turned to the parish clerk.

'I was talking an immense deal with him, that's true, half an hour ago,' replied that ecclesiastic, as one of whom it was no erroneous supposition that he should be on intimate terms with another of the cloth. 'But he didn't say he would be late.'

The discussion was cut off by the appearance round the corner of the van of rays from the curate's spectacles, followed hastily by his face and a few white whiskers, and the swinging tails of his long gaunt coat. Nobody reproached him, seeing how he was reproaching himself; and he entered breathlessly and took his seat.

'Now be we all here?' said the carrier again. They started a second time, and moved on till they were about three hundred yards out of the town, and had nearly reached the second bridge, behind which, as every native remembers, the road takes a turn, and travellers by this highway disappear finally from the view of gazing burghers.

'Well, as I'm alive!' cried the postmistress from the interior of the conveyance, peering through the little square back-window along the road townward.

'What?' said the carrier.

'A man hailing us!'

Another sudden stoppage. 'Somebody else?' the carrier asked.

'Ay, sure!' All waited silently, while those who could gaze out did so.

'Now, who can that be?' Burthen continued. 'I just put it to ye, neighbours, can any man keep time with such hindrances? Bain't we full a'ready? Who in the world can the man be?'

'He's a sort of gentleman,' said the schoolmaster, his position commanding the road more comfortably than that of his comrades.

The stranger, who had been holding up his umbrella to attract their notice, was walking forward leisurely enough, now that he found, by their stopping, that it had been secured. His clothes were decidedly not of a local cut, though it was difficult to point out any particular mark of difference. In his left hand he carried a small leather travelling-bag. As soon as he had overtaken the van he glanced at the inscription on its side, as if to assure himself that he had hailed the right conveyance, and asked if they had room.

The carrier replied that though they were pretty well laden he supposed they could carry one more, whereupon the stranger mounted, and took the seat cleared for him within. And then the horses made another move, this time for good, and swung along with their burden of fourteen souls all told.

'You bain't one of these parts, sir?' said the carrier. 'I could tell that as far as I could see 'ee.'

'Yes, I am one of these parts,' said the stranger.

'Oh? H'm.'

The silence which followed seemed to imply a doubt of the truth of the new-comer's assertion. 'I was speaking of Upper Longpuddle, more particular,' continued the carrier hardily, 'and I think I know most faces of that valley.'

'I was born at Longpuddle, and nursed at Longpuddle, and my father and grandfather before me,' said the passenger quietly.

'Why, to be sure,' said the aged groceress in the background, 'it isn't John Lackland's son – never –it can't be – he who went to foreign parts five-and-thirty years ago with his wife and family? Yet – what do I hear? – that's his father's voice!'

'That's the man,' replied the stranger. 'John Lackland was my father, and I am John Lackland's son. Five-and-thirty years ago, when I was a boy of eleven, my parents emigrated across the seas, taking me and my sister with them. Kytes's boy Tony was the one who drove us and our belongings to Casterbridge on the morning we left; and his was the last Longpuddle face I saw. We sailed the same week across the ocean, and there we've been ever since, and there I've left those I went with – all three.'

'Alive or dead?'

'Dead,' he replied in a low voice. 'And I have come back to the old place, having nourished a thought – not a definite intention, but just a thought – that I should like to return here in a year or two, to spend the remainder of my days.'

'Married man, Mr. Lackland?'

'No.'

'And have the world used 'ee well, sir – or rather John, knowing 'ee as a child? In these rich new countries that we hear of so much, you've got rich with the rest?'

'I am not very rich,' Mr. Lackland said. 'Even in new countries, you know, there are failures. The race is not always to the swift, nor the battle to the strong; and even if it sometimes is, you may be neither swift nor strong. However, that's enough about me. Now, having answered your inquiries, you must answer mine; for being in London, I have come down here entirely to discover what Longpuddle is looking like, and who are living there. That was why I preferred a seat in your van to hiring a carriage for driving across.'

'Well, as for Longpuddle, we rub on there much as usual. Old figures have dropped out o' their frames, so to speak it, and new ones have been put in their places. You mentioned Tony Kytes as having been the one to drive your family and your goods to Casterbridge in his father's waggon when you left. Tony is, I believe, living still, but not at Longpuddle. He went away and settled at Lewgate, near Mellstock, after his marriage. Ah, Tony was a sort o' man!'

'His character had hardly come out when I knew him.'

'No. But 'twas well enough, as far as that goes – except as to women. I shall never forget his courting – never!'

The returned villager waited silently, and the carrier went on: –

Tony Kytes, the Arch-Deceiver

'I SHALL never forget Tony's face. 'Twas a little, round, firm, tight face, with a seam here and there left by the smallpox, but not enough to hurt his looks in a woman's eye, though he'd had it badish when he was a boy. So very serious looking and unsmiling 'a was, that young man, that it really seemed as if he couldn't laugh at all without great pain to his conscience. He looked very hard at a small speck in your eye when talking to 'ee. And there was no more sign of a whisker or beard on Tony Kytes's face than on the palm of my hand. He used to sing "The Tailor's Breeches" with a religious manner, as if it were a hymn: –

' "O the petticoats went off, and the breeches they went on!"
and all the rest of the scandalous stuff. He was quite the women's favourite, and in return for their likings he loved 'em in shoals.

'But in course of time Tony got fixed down to one in particular, Milly Richards, a nice, light, small, tender little thing; and it was soon said that they were engaged to be married. One Saturday he had been to market to do business for his father, and was driving home the waggon in the afternoon. When he reached the foot of the very hill we shall be going over in ten minutes who should he see waiting for him at the top but Unity Sallet, a handsome girl, one of the young women he'd been very tender towards before he'd got engaged to Milly.

'As soon as Tony came up to her she said, "My dear Tony, will you give me a lift home?"

' "That I will, darling," said Tony. "You don't suppose I could refuse 'ee?"

'She smiled a smile, and up she hopped, and on drove Tony.

' "Tony," she says, in a sort of tender chide, "why did ye desert me for that other one? In what is she better than I? I should have made 'ee a finer wife, and a more loving one, too. 'Tisn't girls that are so easily won at first that are the best. Think how long we've known each other – ever since we were children almost – now haven't we, Tony?"

' "Yes, that we have," says Tony, a-struck with the truth o't.

' "And you've never seen anything in me to complain of, have ye, Tony? Now tell the truth to me!"

' "I never have, upon my life," says Tony.

' "And – can you say I'm not pretty, Tony? Now look at me!"

'He let his eyes light upon her for a long while. "I really can't," says he. "In fact, I never knowed you was so pretty before!"

' "Prettier than she?"

'What Tony would have said to that nobody knows, for before he could speak, what should he see ahead, over the hedge past the turning, but a feather he knew well – the feather in Milly's hat – she to whom he had been thinking of putting the question as to giving out the banns that very week.

' "Unity," says he, as mild as he could, "here's Milly coming. Now I shall catch it mightily if she sees 'ee riding here with me; and if you get down she'll be turning the corner in a moment, and, seeing 'ee in the road, she'll know we've been coming on together. Now, dearest Unity, will ye, to avoid all unpleasantness, which I know ye can't bear any more than I, will ye lie down in the back part of the waggon, and let me cover you over with the tarpaulin till Milly has passed? It will all be done in a minute. Do! – and I'll think over what we've said, and perhaps I shall put a loving question to you after all, instead of to Milly. 'Tisn't true that it is all settled between her and me."

'Well, Unity Sallet agreed, and lay down at the back end of the waggon, and Tony covered her over, so that the waggon seemed to be empty but for the loose tarpaulin; and then he drove on to meet Milly.

' "My dear Tony!" cries Milly, looking up with a little pout at him as he came near. "How long you've been coming home! Just as if I didn't live at Upper Longpuddle at all! And I've come to meet you as you asked me to do, and to ride back with you, and talk over our future home since you asked me, and I promised. But I shouldn't have come else, Mr. Tony!"

' "Ay, my dear, I did ask 'ee – to be sure I did, now I think of it – but I had quite forgot it. To ride back with me, did you say, dear Milly?"

' "Well, of course! What can I do else? Surely you don't want me to walk, now I've come all this way?"

' "Oh no, no! I was thinking you might be going on to town to meet your mother. I saw her there – and she looked as if she might be expecting 'ee."

' "Oh no; she's just home. She came across the fields, and so got back before you."

' "Ah! I didn't know that," says Tony. And there was no help for it but to take her up beside him.

'They talked on very pleasantly, and looked at the trees, and beasts, and birds, and insects, and at the ploughmen at work in the fields, till presently who should they see looking out of the upper window of a house that stood beside the road they were following, but Hannah Jolliver, another young beauty of the place at that time, and the very first woman that Tony had fallen in love with – before Milly and before Unity, in fact – the one that he had almost arranged to marry instead of Milly. She was a much more dashing girl than Milly Richards, though he'd not thought much of her of late. The house Hannah was looking from was her aunt's.

' "My dear Milly – my coming wife, as I may call 'ee," says Tony in his modest way, and not so loud that Unity could overhear, "I see a young woman a-looking out of window, who I think may accost me. The fact is, Milly, she had a notion that I was wishing to marry her, and since she's discovered I've promised another, and a prettier than she, I'm rather afeared of her temper if she sees us together. Now, Milly, would you do me a favour – my coming wife, as I may say?"

' "Certainly, dearest Tony," says she.

' "Then would ye creep under the empty sacks just here in front of the waggon, and hide there out of sight till we've passed the house? She hasn't seen us yet. You see, we ought to live in peace and goodwill since 'tis almost Christmas, and 'twill prevent angry passions rising, which we always should do."

' "I don't mind, to oblige you, Tony," Milly said; and though she didn't care much about doing it, she crept under, and crouched down just behind the seat, Unity being snug at the other end. So they drove on till they got near the road-side cottage. Hannah had soon seen him coming, and waited at the window, looking down upon him. She tossed her head a little disdainful and smiled off-hand.

' "Well, aren't you going to be civil enough to ask me to ride home with you!" she says, seeing that he was for driving past with a nod and a smile.

' "Ah, to be sure! What was I thinking of?" said Tony, in a flutter. "But you seem as if you was staying at your aunt's?"

' "No, I am not," she said. "Don't you see I have my bonnet and jacket on? I have only called to see her on my way home. How can you be so stupid, Tony?"

' "In that case – ah – of course you must come along wi' me," says Tony, feeling a dim sort of sweat rising up inside his clothes. And he reined in the horse, and waited till she'd come downstairs, and then helped her up beside him, her feet outside. He drove on again, his face as long as a face that was a round one by nature well could be.

'Hannah looked round sideways into his eyes. "This is nice, isn't it, Tony?" she says. "I like riding with you."

'Tony looked back into her eyes. "And I with you," he said after a while. In short, having considered her, he warmed up, and the more he looked at her the more he liked her, till he couldn't for the life of him think why he had ever said a word about marriage to Milly or Unity while Hannah Jolliver was in question. So they sat a little closer and closer, their feet upon the foot-board and their shoulders touching, and Tony thought over and over again how handsome Hannah was. He spoke tenderer and tenderer, and called her "dear Hannah" in a whisper at last.

' "You've settled it with Milly by this time, I suppose?" said she.

' "N-no, not exactly."

' "What? How low you talk, Tony."

' "Yes – I've a kind of hoarseness. I said, not exactly."

' "I suppose you mean to?"

' "Well, as to that—" His eyes rested on her face, and hers on his. He wondered how he could have been such a fool as not to follow up Hannah. "My sweet Hannah!" he bursts out, taking her hand, not being really able to help it, and forgetting Milly and Unity, and all the world besides. "Settled it? I don't think I have!"

' "Hark!" says Hannah.

' "What?" says Tony, letting go her hand.

' "Surely I heard a sort of little screaming squeak under those sacks? Why, you've been carrying corn, and there's mice in this waggon, I declare!" She began to haul up the tails of her gown.

' "Oh no, 'tis the axle," said Tony in an assuring way. "It do go like that sometimes in dry weather."

' "Perhaps it was. . . . Well, now, to be quite honest, dear Tony, do you like her better than me? Because – because, although I've held off so independent, I'll own at last that I do like 'ee, Tony, to tell the truth; and I wouldn't say no if you asked me – you know what."

'Tony was so won over by this pretty offering mood of a girl who had been quite the reverse (Hannah had a backward way with her at times, if you can mind) that he just glanced behind, and then whispered very soft, "I haven't quite promised her, and I think I can get out of it, and ask you that question you speak of."

' "Throw over Milly? – all to marry me! How delightful!" broke out Hannah, quite loud, clapping her hands.

'At this there was a real squeak – an angry, spiteful squeak, and afterward a long moan, as if something had broke its heart, and a movement of the empty sacks.

' "Something's there!" said Hannah, starting up.

' "It's nothing really," says Tony in a soothing voice, and praying inwardly for a way out of this. "I wouldn't tell 'ee at first, because I wouldn't frighten 'ee. But, Hannah, I've really a couple of ferrets in a bag under there, for rabbiting, and they quarrel sometimes. I don't wish it knowed, as 'twould be called poaching. Oh, they can't get out, bless 'ee – you are quite safe! And – and – what a fine day it is, isn't it, Hannah, for this time of year? Be you going to market next Saturday? How is your aunt now?" And so on, says Tony, to keep her from talking any more about love in Milly's hearing.

'But he found his work cut out for him, and wondering again how he should get out of this ticklish business, he looked about for a chance. Nearing home he saw his father in a field not far off, holding up his hand as if he wished to speak to Tony.

' "Would you mind taking the reins a moment, Hannah," he said, much relieved, "while I go and find out what father wants?"

'She consented, and away he hastened into the field, only too glad to get breathing time. He found that his father was looking at him with rather a stern eye.

'"Come, come, Tony," says old Mr. Kytes, as soon as his son was alongside him, "this won't do, you know."

'"What?" says Tony.

'"Why, if you mean to marry Milly Richards, do it, and there's an end o't. But don't go driving about the country with Jolliver's daughter and making a scandal. I won't have such things done."

'"I only asked her – that is, she asked me, to ride home."

'"She? Why, now, if it had been Milly, 'twould have been quite proper; but you and Hannah Jolliver going about by yourselves —"

'"Milly's there, too, father."

'"Milly? Where?"

'"Under the corn-sacks! Yes, the truth is, father, I've got rather into a nunnywatch, I'm afeared! Unity Sallet is there, too – yes, at the other end, under the tarpaulin. All three are in that waggon, and what to do with 'em I know no more than the dead! The best plan is, as I'm thinking, to speak out loud and plain to one of 'em before the rest, and that will settle it; not but what 'twill cause 'em to kick up a bit of a miff, for certain. Now which would you marry, father, if you was in my place?"

'"Whichever of 'em did *not* ask to ride with thee."

'"That was Milly, I'm bound to say, as she only mounted by my invitation. But Milly –"

'"Then stick to Milly, she's the best. . . . But look at that!"

'His father pointed toward the waggon. "She can't hold that horse in. You shouldn't have left the reins in her hands. Run on and take the horse's head, or there'll be some accident to them maids!"

'Tony's horse, in fact, in spite of Hannah's tugging at the reins, had started on his way at a brisk walking pace, being very anxious to get back to the stable, for he had had a long day out. Without another word Tony rushed away from his father to overtake the horse.

'Now of all things that could have happened to wean him from Milly there was nothing so powerful as his father's recommending her. No; it could not be Milly, after all. Hannah must be the one, since he could not marry all three as he longed to do. This he thought while running after the waggon. But queer things were happening inside it.

'It was, of course, Milly who had screamed under the sack-bags, being obliged to let off her bitter rage and shame in that way at what Tony was saying, and never daring to show, for very pride and dread o' being laughed at, that she was in hiding. She became more and more restless, and in twisting herself about, what did she see but another woman's foot and white stocking close to her head. It quite frightened her, not knowing that Unity Sallet was in the waggon likewise. But after the fright was over she determined to get to the bottom of all this, and she crept and crept along the bed of the waggon, under the tarpaulin, like a snake, when lo and behold she came face to face with Unity.

'"Well, if this isn't disgraceful!" says Milly in a raging whisper to Unity.

'"Tis," says Unity, "to see you hiding in a young man's waggon like this, and no great character belonging to either of ye!"

'"Mind what you are saying!" replied Milly, getting louder. "I am engaged to be married to him, and haven't I a right to be here? What right have you, I should like to know? What has he been promising you? A pretty lot of nonsense, I expect! But what Tony says to other women is all mere wind, and no concern to me!"

'"Don't you be too sure!" says Unity. "He's going to have Hannah, and not you, nor me either; I could hear that."

'Now at these strange voices sounding from under the cloth Hannah was thunderstruck a'most into a swound; and it was just at this time that the horse moved on. Hannah tugged away wildly, not knowing what she was doing; and as the quarrel rose louder and louder Hannah got so horrified that she let go the reins altogether. The horse went on at his own pace, and coming to the corner where we turn round to drop down the hill to Lower Longpuddle he turned too quick, the off wheels went up the bank, the waggon rose sideways till it was quite on edge upon the near axles, and out rolled the three maidens into the road in a heap. The horse looked round and stood still.

'When Tony came up, frightened and breathless, he was relieved enough to see that neither of his darlings was hurt, beyond a few scratches from the brambles of the hedge. But he was rather alarmed when he heard how they were going on at one another.

'"Don't ye quarrel, my dears – don't ye!" says he, taking off his hat out of respect to 'em. And then he would have kissed them all round, as fair and square as a man could, but they were in too much of a taking to let him, and screeched and sobbed till they was quite spent.

'"Now I'll speak out honest, because I ought to," says Tony, as soon as he could get heard. "And this is the truth," says he. "I've asked Hannah to be mine, and she is willing, and we are going to put up the banns next—"

'Tony had not noticed that Hannah's father was coming up behind, nor had he noticed that Hannah's face was beginning to bleed from the scratch of a bramble. Hannah had seen her father, and had run to him, crying worse than ever.

'"My daughter is *not* willing, sir!" says Mr. Jolliver hot and strong. "Be you willing, Hannah? I ask ye to have spirit enough to refuse him, if yer virtue is left to 'ee and you run no risk?"

'"She's as sound as a bell for me, that I'll swear!" says Tony, flaring up. "And so's the others, come to that, though you may think it an onusual thing in me!"

'"I have spirit, and I do refuse him!" says Hannah, partly because her father was there, and partly, too, in a tantrum because of the discovery, and the scar that might be left on her face. "Little did I think when I was so soft with him just now that I was talking to such a false deceiver!"

'"What, you won't have me, Hannah?" says Tony, his jaw hanging down like a dead man's.

'"Never – I would sooner marry no – nobody at all!" she gasped out, though with her heart in her throat, for she would not have refused Tony if he had asked her quietly, and her father had not been there, and her face had not been scratched by the bramble. And having said that, away she walked upon her father's arm, thinking and hoping he would ask her again.

'Tony didn't know what to say next. Milly was sobbing her heart out; but as his father had strongly recommended her he couldn't feel inclined that way. So he turned to Unity.

'"Well, will you, Unity dear, be mine?" he says.

'"Take her leavings? Not I!" says Unity. "I'd scorn it!" And away walks Unity Sallet likewise, though she looked back when she'd gone some way, to see if he was following her.

'So there at last were left Milly and Tony by themselves, she crying in watery streams, and Tony looking like a tree struck by lightning.

'"Well, Milly," he says at last, going up to her, "it do seem as if fate has ordained that it should be you and I, or nobody. And what must be must be, I suppose. Hey, Milly?"

'"If you like, Tony. You didn't really mean what you said to them?"

'"Not a word of it!" declares Tony, bringing down his fist upon his palm.

'And then he kissed her, and put the waggon to rights, and they mounted together; and their banns were put up the very next Sunday. I was not able to go to their wedding, but it was a rare party they had, by all account. Everybody in Longpuddle was there almost; you among the rest, I think, Mr. Flaxton?' The speaker turned to the parish clerk.

'I was,' said Mr. Flaxton. 'And that party was the cause of a very curious change in some other people's affairs; I mean in Steve Hardcome's and his cousin James's.'

'Ah! the Hardcomes,' said the stranger. 'How familiar that name is to me! What of them?'

The clerk cleared his throat and began: –

The History of the Hardcomes

'Yes, Tony's was the very best wedding-randy that ever I was at; and I've been at a good many, as you may suppose' – turning to the newly-arrived one – 'having, as a church-officer, the privilege to attend all christening, wedding, and funeral parties – such being our Wessex custom.

' 'Twas on a frosty night in Christmas week, and among the folk invited were the said Hardcomes o' Climmerston – Steve and James – first cousins, both of them small farmers, just entering into business on their own account. With them came, as a matter of course, their intended wives, two young women of the neighbourhood, both very pretty and sprightly maidens, and numbers of friends from Abbot's-Cernel, and Weatherbury, and Mellstock, and I don't know where – a regular houseful.

'The kitchen was cleared of furniture for dancing, and the old folk played at "Put" and "All-fours"* in the parlour, though at last they gave that up to join in the dance. The top of the figure was by the large front window of the room, and there were so many couples that the lower part of the figure reached through the door at the back, and into the darkness of the out-house; in fact, you couldn't see the end of the row at all, and 'twas never known exactly how long that dance was, the lowest couples being lost among the faggots and brushwood in the out-house.

'When we had danced a few hours, and the crowns of we taller men were swelling into lumps with bumping the beams of the ceiling, the first fiddler laid down his fiddle-bow, and said he should play no more, for he wished to dance. And in another hour the second fiddler laid down his, and said he wanted to dance, too; so there was only the third fiddler left, and he was a' old, veteran man, very weak in the wrist. However, he managed to keep up a faltering tweedle-dee; but there being no chair in the room, and his knees being as weak as his wrists, he was obliged to sit upon as much of the little corner-table as projected beyond the corner-cupboard fixed over it, which was not a very wide seat for a man advanced in years.

'Among those who danced most continually were the two engaged couples, as was natural to their situation. Each pair was very well matched, and very unlike the other. James Hardcome's intended was called Emily Darth, and both she and James were gentle, nice-minded, in-door people, fond of a quiet life. Steve and his chosen, named Olive

---

* "Put" and "All-fours": card games

Pawle, were different; they were of a more bustling nature, fond of racketing about and seeing what was going on in the world. The two couples had arranged to get married on the same day, and that not long thence; Tony's wedding being a sort of stimulant, as is often the case; I've noticed it professionally many times.

'They danced with such a will as only young people in that stage of courtship can dance; and it happened that as the evening wore on James had for his partner Stephen's plighted one, Olive, at the same time that Stephen was dancing with James's Emily. It was noticed that in spite o' the exchange the young men seemed to enjoy the dance no less than before. By and by they were treading another tune in the same changed order as we had noticed earlier, and though at first each one had held the other's mistress strictly at half-arm's length, lest there should be shown any objection to too close quarters by the lady's proper man, as time passed there was a little more closeness between 'em; and presently a little more closeness still.

'The later it got the more did each of the two cousins dance with the wrong young girl, and the tighter did he hold her to his side as he whirled her round; and, what was very remarkable, neither seemed to mind what the other was doing. The party began to draw towards its end, and I saw no more that night, being one of the first to leave, on account of my morning's business. But I learnt the rest of it from those that knew.

'After finishing a particularly warming dance with the changed partners, as I've mentioned, the two young men looked at one another, and in a moment or two went out into the porch together.

' "James," says Steve, "what were you thinking of when you were dancing with my Olive?"

' "Well," said James, "perhaps what you were thinking of when you were dancing with my Emily."

' "I was thinking," said Steve with some hesitation, "that I wouldn't mind changing for good and all!"

' "It was what I was feeling likewise," said James.

' "I willingly agree to it, if you think we could manage it."

' "So do I. But what would the girls say?"

' " 'Tis my belief," said Steve, "that they wouldn't particularly object. Your Emily clung as close to me as if she already belonged to me, dear girl."

' "And your Olive to me," says James. "I could feel her heart beating like a clock."

'Well, they agreed to put it to the girls when they were all four walking home together. And they did so. When they parted that night the exchange was decided on – all having been done under the hot excitement of that evening's dancing. Thus it happened that on the following Sunday morning, when the people were sitting in church with mouths wide open to hear the names published as they had expected, there was no small amazement to hear them coupled the wrong way, as it seemed. The congregation whispered, and thought the parson had made a mistake; till they discovered that his reading of the names was verily the true way. As they had decided, so they were married, each one to the other's original property.

'Well, the two couples lived on for a year or two ordinarily enough, till the time came when these young people began to grow a little less warm to their respective spouses, as is the rule of married life; and the two cousins wondered more and more in their hearts what had made 'em so mad at the last moment to marry crosswise as they did, when they might have married straight, as was planned by Nature, and as they had fallen in love. 'Twas Tony's party that had done it, plain enough, and they half wished they had never gone there. James, being a quiet, fireside, perusing man, felt at times a wide gap between himself and Olive, his wife, who loved riding and driving and outdoor jaunts to a degree; while Steve, who was always knocking about hither and thither, had a very domestic wife, who worked samplers, and made hearthrugs, scarcely ever wished to cross the threshold, and only drove out with him to please him.

'However, they said very little about this mismating to any of their acquaintances, though sometimes Steve would look at James's wife, and sigh, and James would look at Steve's wife and do the same. Indeed, at last the two men were frank enough towards each other not to mind mentioning it quietly to themselves, in a long-faced, sorry-smiling, whimsical sort of way, and would shake their heads together over their foolishness in upsetting a well-considered choice on the strength of an hour's fancy in the whirl and wildness of a dance. Still, they were sensible and honest young fellows enough, and did their best to make shift with their lot as they had arranged it, and not to repine at what could not now be altered or mended.

'So things remained till one fine summer day they went for their yearly little outing together, as they had made it their custom to do for a long while past. This year they chose Budmouth-Regis as the place to spend their holiday in; and off they went in their best clothes at nine o'clock in the morning.

'When they had reached Budmouth-Regis they walked two and two along the shore – their new boots going squeakity-squash upon the clammy velvet sands. I can seem to see 'em now! Then they looked at the ships in the harbour; and then went up to the Look-out; and then had dinner at an inn, and then again walked two and two, squeakity-squash, upon the velvet sands. As evening drew on they sat on one of the public seats upon the Esplanade, and listened to the band; and then they said, "What shall we do next?"

' "Of all things," said Olive (Mrs. James Hardcome, that is), "I should like to row in the bay! We could listen to the music from the water as well as from here, and have the fun of rowing besides."

' "The very thing; so should I," says Stephen, his tastes being always like hers.'

Here the clerk turned to the curate.

'But you, sir, know the rest of the strange particulars of that strange evening of their lives better than anybody else, having had much of it from their own lips, which I had not; and perhaps you'll oblige the gentleman?'

'Certainly, if it is wished,' said the curate. And he took up the clerk's tale: –

'Stephen's wife hated the sea, except from land, and couldn't bear the thought of going into a boat. James, too, disliked the water, and said that for his part he would much sooner stay on and listen to the band in the seat they occupied, though he did not wish to stand in his wife's way if she desired a row. The end of the discussion was that James and his cousin's wife Emily agreed to remain where they were sitting and enjoy the music, while they watched the other two hire a boat just beneath, and take their water-excursion of half an hour or so, till they should choose to come back and join the sitters on the Esplanade; when they would all start homeward together.

'Nothing could have pleased the other two restless ones better than this arrangement; and Emily and James watched them go down to the boatman below and choose one of the little yellow skiffs, and walk carefully out upon the little plank that was laid on trestles to enable them to get alongside the craft. They saw Stephen hand Olive in, and take his seat facing her; when they were settled they waved their hands to the couple watching them, and then Stephen took the pair of sculls and pulled off to the tune beat by the band, she steering through the other boats skimming about, for the sea was as smooth as glass that evening, and pleasure-seekers were rowing everywhere.

' "How pretty they look moving on, don't they?" said Emily to James (as I've been assured). "They both enjoy it equally. In everything their likings are the same."

' "That's true," said James.

' "They would have made a handsome pair if they had married," said she.

' "Yes," said he. " 'Tis a pity we should have parted 'em."

' "Don't talk of that, James," said she. "For better or for worse we decided to do as we did, and there's an end of it."

'They sat on after that without speaking, side by side, and the band played as before; the people strolled up and down; and Stephen and Olive shrank smaller and smaller as they shot straight out to sea. The two on shore used to relate how they saw Stephen stop rowing a moment, and take off his coat to get at his work better; but James's wife sat quite still in the stern, holding the tiller-ropes by which she steered the boat. When they had got very small indeed she turned her head to shore.

' "She is waving her handkerchief to us," said Stephen's wife, who thereupon pulled out her own, and waved it as a return signal.

'The boat's course had been a little awry while Mrs. James neglected her steering to wave her handkerchief to her husband and Mrs. Stephen; but now the light skiff went straight onward again, and they could soon see nothing more of the two figures it contained than Olive's light mantle and Stephen's white shirt-sleeves behind.

'The two on the shore talked on. " 'Twas very curious – our changing partners at Tony Kytes's wedding," Emily declared. "Tony was of a fickle nature by all account, and it really seemed as if his character had infected us that night. Which of you two was it that first proposed not to marry as we were engaged?"

' "H'm – I can't remember at this moment," says James. "We talked it over, you know; and no sooner said than done."

' " 'Twas the dancing," said she. "People get quite crazy sometimes in a dance."

' "They do," he owned. ' "James – do you think they care for one another still?" asks Mrs. Stephen.

'James Hardcome mused and admitted that perhaps a little tender feeling might flicker up in their hearts for a moment now and then. "Still, nothing of any account," he said.

' "I sometimes think that Olive is in Steve's mind a good deal," murmurs Mrs. Stephen; "particularly when she pleases his fancy by riding past our window at a gallop on one of the draught-horses. . . . I never could do anything of that sort; I could never get over my fear of a horse."

' "And I am no horseman, though I pretend to be on her account," murmured James Hardcome. "But isn't it almost time for them to turn and sweep round to the shore, as the other boating folk have done? I wonder what Olive means by steering away straight to the horizon like that? She has hardly swerved from a direct line seaward since they started."

' "No doubt they are talking, and don't think of where they are going," suggests Stephen's wife.

' "Perhaps so," said James. "I didn't know Steve could row like that."

' "Oh yes," says she. "He often comes here on business, and generally has a pull round the bay."

' "I can hardly see the boat or them," says James again; "and it is getting dark."

'The heedless pair afloat now formed a mere speck in the films of the coming night, which thickened apace, till it completely swallowed up their distant shapes. They had disappeared while still following the same straight course away from the world of land-livers, as if they were intending to drop over the sea-edge into space, and never return to earth again.

'The two on the shore continued to sit on, punctually abiding by their agreement to remain on the same spot till the others returned. The Esplanade lamps were lit one by one, the bandsmen folded up their stands and departed, the yachts in the bay hung out their riding lights, and the little boats came back to shore one after another, their hirers walking on to the sands by the plank they had climbed to go afloat; but among these Stephen and Olive did not appear.

' "What a time they are!" said Emily. "I am getting quite chilly. I did not expect to have to sit so long in the evening air."

'Thereupon James Hardcome said that he did not require his overcoat, and insisted on lending it to her.

'He wrapped it round Emily's shoulders.

' "Thank you, James," she said. "How cold Olive must be in that thin jacket!"

'He said he was thinking so, too. "Well, they are sure to be quite close at hand by this time, though we can't see 'em. The boats are not all in yet. Some of the rowers are fond of paddling along the shore to finish out their hour of hiring."

' "Shall we walk by the edge of the water," said she, "to see if we can discover them?"

'He assented, reminding her that they must not lose sight of the seat, lest the belated pair should return and miss them, and be vexed that they had not kept the appointment.

'They walked a sentry-beat up and down the sands immediately opposite the seat; and still the others did not come. James Hardcome at last went to the boatman, thinking that after all his wife and cousin might have come in under shadow of the dusk without being perceived, and might have forgotten the appointment at the bench.

' "All in?" asked James.

'"All but one boat," said the lessor. "I can't think where that couple is keeping to. They might run foul of something or other in the dark."

'Again Stephen's wife and Olive's husband waited, with more and more anxiety. But no little yellow boat returned. Was it possible they could have landed further down the Esplanade?

'"It may have been done to escape paying," said the boat-owner. "But they didn't look like people who would do that."

'James Hardcome knew that he could found no hope on such a reason as that. But now, remembering what had been casually discussed between Steve and himself about their wives from time to time, he admitted for the first time the possibility that their old tenderness had been revived by their face-to-face position more strongly than either had anticipated at starting – the excursion having been so obviously undertaken for the pleasure of the performance only – and that they had landed at some steps he knew of further down towards the pier, to be longer alone together.

'Still he disliked to harbour the thought, and would not mention its existence to his companion. He merely said to her, "Let us walk further on."

'They did so, and lingered between the boat-stage and the pier till Stephen Hardcome's wife was uneasy, and was obliged to accept James's offered arm. Thus the night advanced. Emily was presently so worn out by fatigue that James felt it necessary to conduct her home; there was, too, a remote chance that the truants had landed in the harbour on the other side of the town, or elsewhere, and hastened home in some unexpected way, in the belief that their consorts would not have waited so long.

'However, he left a direction in the town that a look-out should be kept, though this was arranged privately, the bare possibility of an elopement being enough to make him reticent; and, full of misgivings, the two remaining ones hastened to catch the last train out of Budmouth Regis; and when they got to Casterbridge drove back to Upper Longpuddle.'

'Along this very road as we do now,' remarked the parish clerk.

'To be sure – along this very road,' said the curate. 'However, Stephen and Olive were not at their homes; neither had entered the village since leaving it in the morning. Emily and James Hardcome went to their respective dwellings to snatch a hasty night's rest, and at daylight the next morning they drove again to Casterbridge and entered the Budmouth train, the line being just opened.

'Nothing had been heard of the couple there during this brief absence. In the course of a few hours some young men testified to having seen such a man and woman rowing in a frail hired craft, the head of the boat kept straight to sea; they had sat looking in each other's faces as if they were in a dream, with no consciousness of what they were doing, or whither they were steering. It was not till late that day that more tidings reached James's ears. The boat had been found drifting bottom upward a long way from land. In the evening the sea rose somewhat, and a cry spread through the town that two bodies were cast ashore in Lulwind Bay, several miles to the eastward. They were brought to Budmouth, and inspection revealed them to be the missing pair. It was said that they had been found tightly locked in each other's arms, his lips upon hers, their features still wrapt in the same calm and dream-like repose which had been observed in their demeanour as they had glided along.

'Neither James nor Emily questioned the original motives of the unfortunate man and woman in putting to sea. They were both above suspicion as to intention. Whatever their mutual feelings might have led them on to, underhand behaviour at starting was foreign to the nature of either. Conjecture pictured that they might have fallen into tender reverie while gazing each into a pair of eyes that had formerly flashed for him and her alone, and, unwilling to avow what their mutual sentiments were, they had done no more than continue thus, oblivious of time and space, till darkness suddenly overtook them far from land. But nothing was truly known. It had been their destiny to die thus. The two halves, intended by Nature to make the perfect whole, had failed in that result during their lives, though "in their death they were not divided". Their bodies were brought home, and buried on one day. I remember that, on looking round the churchyard while reading the service, I observed nearly all the parish at their funeral.'

'It was so, sir,' said the clerk.

'The remaining two,' continued the curate (whose voice had grown husky while relating the lovers' sad fate), 'were a more thoughtful and far-seeing, though less romantic, couple than the first. They were now mutually bereft of a companion, and found themselves by this accident in a position to fulfil their destiny according to Nature's plan and their own original and calmly-formed intention. James Hardcome took Emily to wife in the course of a year and a half; and the marriage proved in every respect a happy one. I solemnized the service, Hardcome having told me, when he came to give notice of the proposed wedding, the story of his first wife's loss almost word for word as I have told it to you.'

'And are they living in Longpuddle still?' asked the new-comer.

'Oh no, sir,' interposed the clerk. 'James has been dead these dozen years, and his mis'ess about six or seven. They had no children. William Privett used to be their odd man till he died.'

'Ah – William Privett! He dead, too? – dear me?' said the other. 'All passed away!'

'Yes, sir. William was much older than I. He'd ha' been over eighty if he had lived till now.'

'There was something very strange about William's death – very strange indeed!' sighed a melancholy man in the back of the van. It was the seedsman's father, who had hitherto kept silence.

'And what might that have been?' asked Mr. Lackland.

The Superstitious Man's Story

'WILLIAM, as you may know, was a curious, silent man; you could feel when he came near 'ee; and if he was in the house or anywhere behind your back without your seeing him, there seemed to be something clammy in the air, as if a cellar door was opened close by your elbow. Well, one Sunday, at a time that William was in very good health to all appearance, the bell that was ringing for church went very heavy all of a sudden; the sexton, who told me o't, said he'd not known the bell go so heavy in his hand for years – and he feared it meant a death in the parish. That was on the Sunday, as I say. During the week after, it chanced that William's wife was staying up late one night to finish her ironing, she doing the washing for Mr. and Mrs. Hardcome. Her husband had finished his supper and gone to bed as usual some hour or two before. While she ironed she heard him coming downstairs; he stopped to put on his boots at the stair-foot, where he always left them, and then came on into the living-room where she was ironing, passing through it towards the door, this being the only way from the staircase to the outside of the house. No word was said on either side, William not being a man given to much speaking, and his wife being occupied with her work. He went out and closed the door behind him. As her husband had now and then gone out in this way at night before when unwell, or unable to sleep for want of a pipe, she took no particular notice, and continued at her ironing. This she finished shortly after, and as he had not come in she waited a while for him, putting away the irons and things, and preparing the table for his breakfast in the morning. Still he did not return, and supposing him not far off, and wanting to get to bed herself, tired as she was, she left the door unbarred and went to the stairs, after writing on the back of the door with chalk: *Mind and do the door* (because he was a forgetful man).

'To her great surprise, and I might say alarm, on reaching the foot of the stairs his boots were standing there as they always stood when he had gone to rest; going up to their chamber she found him in bed sleeping as sound as a rock. How he could have got back again without her seeing or hearing him was beyond her comprehension. It could only have been by passing behind her very quietly while she was bumping with the iron. But this notion did not satisfy her: it was surely impossible that she should not have seen him come in through a room so small. She could not unravel the mystery, and felt very queer and uncomfortable about it. However, she would not disturb him to question him then, and went to bed herself.

'He rose and left for his work very early the next morning, before she was awake, and she waited his return to breakfast with much anxiety for an explanation, for thinking over the matter by daylight made it seem only the more startling. When he came in to the meal he said, before she could put her question, "What's the meaning of them words chalked on the door?"

'She told him, and asked him about his going out the night before. William declared that he had never left the bedroom after entering it, having in fact undressed, lain down, and fallen asleep directly, never once waking till the clock struck five, and he rose up to go to his labour.

'Betty Privett was as certain in her own mind that he did go out as she was of her own existence, and was little less certain that he did not return. She felt too disturbed to argue with him, and let the subject drop as though she must have been mistaken. When she was walking down Longpuddle street later in the day she met Jim Weedle's daughter Nancy, and said, "Well, Nancy, you do look sleepy to-day!"

' "Yes, Mrs. Privett," says Nancy. "Now don't tell anybody, but I don't mind letting you know what the reason o't is. Last night, being Old Midsummer Eve, some of us went to church porch, and didn't get home till near one."

' "Did ye?" says Mrs. Privett. "Old Midsummer yesterday, was it? Faith I didn't think whe'r 'twas Midsummer or Michaelmas; I'd too much work to do."

' "Yes. And we were frightened enough, I can tell 'ee, by what we saw."

' "What did ye see?"

'(You may not remember, sir, having gone off to foreign parts so young, that on Midsummer Night it is believed hereabout that the faint shapes of all the folk in the parish who are going to be at death's door within the year can be seen entering the church. Those who get over their illness come out again after a while; those that are doomed to die do not return.)

' "What did you see?" asked William's wife.

' "Well," says Nancy, backwardly – "we needn't tell what we saw, or who we saw."

' "You saw my husband," says Betty Privett, in a quiet way.

' "Well, since you put it so," says Nancy, hanging fire, "we – thought we did see him; but it was darkish, and we was frightened, and of course it might not have been he."

' "Nancy, you needn't mind letting it out, though 'tis kept back in kindness. And he didn't come out of church again: I know it as well as you."

'Nancy did not answer yes or no to that, and no more was said. But three days after, William Privett was mowing with John Chiles in Mr. Hardcome's meadow, and in the heat of the day they sat down to eat their bit o' nunch under a tree, and empty their flagon. Afterwards both of 'em fell asleep as they sat. John Chiles was the first to wake, and as he looked towards his fellow-mower he saw one of those great white miller's-souls as we call 'em – that is to say, a miller-moth – come from William's open mouth while he slept, and fly straight away. John thought it odd enough, as William had worked in a mill for several years when he was a boy. He then looked at the sun, and found by the place o't that they had slept a long while, and as William did not wake, John called to him and said it was high time to begin work again. He took no notice, and then John went up and shook him, and found he was dead.

'Now on that very day old Philip Hookhorn was down at Longpuddle Spring dipping up a pitcher of water; and as he turned away, who should he see coming down to the spring on the other side but William, looking very pale and odd. This surprised Philip Hookhorn very much, for years before that time William's little son – his only child – had been drowned in that spring while at play there, and this had so preyed upon William's mind that he'd never been seen near the spring afterwards, and had been known to go half a mile out of his way to avoid the place. On inquiry, it was found that William in body could not have stood by the spring, being in the mead two miles off; and it also came out that the time at which he was seen at the spring was the very time when he died.'

'A rather melancholy story,' observed the emigrant, after a minute's silence.

'Yes, yes. Well, we must take ups and downs together,' said the seedsman's father.

'You don't know, Mr. Lackland, I suppose, what a rum start that was between Andrey Satchel and Jane Vallens and the pa'son and clerk o' Scrimpton?' said the master-thatcher, a man with a spark of subdued liveliness in his eye, who had hitherto kept his attention mainly upon small objects a long way ahead, as he sat in front of the van with his feet outside. 'Theirs was a queerer experience of a pa'son and clerk than some folks get, and may cheer 'ee up a little after this dampness that's been flung over yer soul.'

The returned one replied that he knew nothing of the history, and should be happy to hear it, quite recollecting the personality of the man Satchel.

'Ah, no; this Andrey Satchel is the son of the Satchel that you knew; this one has not been married more than two or three years, and 'twas at the time o' the wedding that the accident happened that I could tell 'ee of, or anybody else here, for that matter.'

'No, no; you must tell it, neighbour, if anybody,' said several; a request in which Mr. Lackland joined, adding that the Satchel family was one he had known well before leaving home.

'I'll just mention, as you be a stranger,' whispered the carrier to Lackland, 'that Christopher's stories will bear pruning.'

The emigrant nodded.

'Well, I can soon tell it,' said the master-thatcher, schooling himself to a tone of actuality. 'Though as it has more to do with the pa'son and clerk than with Andrey himself, it ought to be told by a better church-man than I.

Andrey Satchel and the Parson and Clerk

'IT ALL arose, you must know, from Andrey being fond of a drop of drink at that time – though he's a sober enough man now by all account, so much the better for him. Jane, his bride, you see, was somewhat older than Andrey; how much older I don't pretend to say; she was not one of our parish, and the register alone may be able to tell that. But, at any rate, her being a little ahead of her young man in mortal years, coupled with other bodily circumstances owing to that young man – '

('Ah, poor thing!' sighed the women.)

' – made her very anxious to get the thing done before he changed his mind; and 'twas with a joyful countenance (they say) that she, with Andrey and his brother and sister-in-law, marched off to church one

November morning as soon as 'twas day a'most to be made one with Andrey for the rest of her life. He had left our place long before it was light, and the folks that were up all waved their lanterns at him, and flung up their hats as he went.

'The church of her parish was a mile and more from where she lived, and, as it was a wonderful fine day for the time of year, the plan was that as soon as they were married they would make out a holiday by driving straight off to Port Bredy, to see the ships and the sea and the sojers, instead of coming back to a meal at the house of the distant relation she lived wi', and moping about there all the afternoon.

'Well, some folks noticed that Andrey walked with rather wambling steps to church that morning; the truth o't was that his nearest neighbour's child had been christened the day before, and Andrey, having stood godfather, had stayed all night keeping up the christening, for he had said to himself, "Not if I live to be a thousand shall I again be made a godfather one day, and a husband the next, and perhaps a father the next, and therefore I'll make the most of the blessing." So that when he started from home in the morning he had not been in bed at all. The result was, as I say, that when he and his bride-to-be walked up the church to get married, the pa'son (who was a very strict man inside the church, whatever he was outside) looked hard at Andrey, and said, very sharp:

'"How's this, my man? You are in liquor. And so early, too. I'm ashamed of you!"

'"Well, that's true, sir," says Andrey. "But I can walk straight enough for practical purposes. I can walk a chalk line," he says (meaning no offence), "as well as some other folk: and" – (getting hotter) – "I reckon that if you, Pa'son Billy Toogood, had kept up a christening all night so thoroughly as I have done, you wouldn't be able to stand at all; d—me if you would!"

'This answer made Pa'son Billy – as they used to call him – rather spitish, not to say hot, for he was a warm-tempered man if provoked, and he said, very decidedly: "Well, I cannot marry you in this state; and I will not! Go home and get sober!" And he slapped the book together like a rat-trap.

'Then the bride burst out crying as if her heart would break, for very fear that she would lose Andrey after all her hard work to get him, and begged and implored the pa'son to go on with the ceremony. But no.

'"I won't be a party to your solemnizing matrimony with a tipsy man," says Mr. Toogood. "It is not right and decent. I am sorry for you, my young woman, seeing the condition you are in, but you'd better go home again. I wonder how you could think of bringing him here drunk like this!"

' "But if – if he don't come drunk he won't come at all, sir!" she says, through her sobs.

' "I can't help that," says the pa'son; and plead as she might, it did not move him. Then she tried him another way.

' "Well, then, if you'll go home, sir, and leave us here, and come back to the church in an hour or two, I'll undertake to say that he shall be as sober as a judge," she cries. "We'll bide here, with your permission; for if he once goes out of this here church unmarried, all Van Amburgh's horses won't drag him back again!"

' "Very well," says the parson. "I'll give you two hours, and then I'll return."

' "And please, sir, lock the door, so that we can't escape!" says she.

' "Yes," says the parson.

' "And let nobody know that we are here."

'The pa'son then took off his clane white surplice, and went away; and the others consulted upon the best means for keeping the matter a secret, which it was not a very hard thing to do, the place being so lonely, and the hour so early. The witnesses, Andrey's brother and brother's wife, neither one o' which cared about Andrey's marrying Jane, and had come rather against their will, said they couldn't wait two hours in that hole of a place, wishing to get home to Longpuddle before dinner-time. They were altogether so crusty that the clerk said there was no difficulty in their doing as they wished. They could go home as if their brother's wedding had actually taken place and the married couple had gone onward for their day's pleasure jaunt to Port Bredy as intended. He, the clerk, and any casual passer-by would act as witnesses when the pa'son came back.

'This was agreed to, and away Andrey's relations went, nothing loath, and the clerk shut the church door and prepared to lock in the couple. The bride went up and whispered to him, with her eyes a-streaming still.

' "My dear good clerk," she says, "if we bide here in the church, folk may see us through the windows, and find out what has happened; and 'twould cause such a talk and scandal that I never should get over it: and perhaps, too, dear Andrey might try to get out and leave me! Will ye lock us up in the tower, my dear good clerk?" she says. "I'll tole* him in there if you will."

'The clerk had no objection to do this to oblige the poor young woman, and they toled Andrey into the tower, and the clerk locked 'em both up straightway, and then went home, to return at the end of the two hours.

'Pa'son Toogood had not been long in his house after leaving the church when he saw a gentleman in pink and top-boots ride past his windows, and with a sudden flash of heat he called to mind that the

---

* tole: (dialect) lure or tempt

hounds met that day just on the edge of his parish. The pa'son was one who dearly loved sport, and much he longed to be there.

'In short, except o' Sundays and at tide-times in the week, Pa'son Billy was the life o' the hunt. 'Tis true that he was poor, and that he rode all of a heap, and that his black mare was rat-tailed and old, and his tops older, and all over of one colour, whitey-brown, and full o' cracks. But he'd been in at the death of three thousand foxes. And – being a bachelor man – every time he went to bed in summer he used to open the bed at bottom and crawl up head foremost, to mind en of the coming winter and the good sport he'd have, and the foxes going to earth. And whenever there was a christening at the Squire's, and he had dinner there afterwards, as he always did, he never failed to christen the chiel over again in a bottle of port wine.

'Now the clerk was the pa'son's groom and gardener and general manager, and had just got back to his work in the garden when he, too, saw the hunting man pass, and presently saw lots more of 'em, noblemen and gentry, and then he saw the hounds, the huntsman, Jim Tread-hedge, the whipper-in, and I don't know who besides. The clerk loved going to cover as frantical as the pa'son, so much so that whenever he saw or heard the pack he could no more rule his feelings than if they were the winds of heaven. He might be bedding, or he might be sowing – all was forgot. So he throws down his spade and rushes in to the pa'son, who was by this time as frantical to go as he.

' "That there mare of yours, sir, do want exercise bad, very bad, this morning!" the clerk says, all of a tremble. "Don't ye think I'd better trot her round the downs for an hour, sir?"

' "To be sure, she does want exercise badly. I'll trot her round myself," says the pa'son.

' "Oh – you'll trot her yerself? Well, there's the cob, sir. Really that cob is getting oncontrollable through biding in a stable so long! If you wouldn't mind my putting on the saddle—"

' "Very well. Take him out, certainly," says the pa'son, never caring what the clerk did so long as he himself could get off immediately. So, scrambling into his riding-boots and breeches as quick as he could, he rode off towards the meet, intending to be back in an hour. No sooner was he gone than the clerk mounted the cob, and was off after him. When the pa'son got to the meet he found a lot of friends, and was as jolly as he could be: the hounds found a'most as soon as they threw off, and there was great excitement. So, forgetting that he had meant to go back at once, away rides the pa'son with the rest o' the hunt, all across the fallow ground that lies between Lippet Wood and Green's Copse; and as he galloped he looked behind for a moment, and there was the clerk close to his heels.

' "Ha, ha, clerk – you here?" he says.
' "Yes, sir, here be I," says t'other.
' "Fine exercise for the horses!"
' "Ay, sir – hee, hee!" says the clerk.

'So they went on and on, into Green's Copse, then across to Higher Jirton; then on across this very turnpike-road to Waterston Ridge, then away towards Yalbury Wood: up hill and down dale, like the very wind, the clerk close to the pa'son, and the pa'son not far from the hounds. Never was there a finer run knowed with that pack than they had that day; and neither pa'son nor clerk thought one word about the unmarried couple locked up in the church tower waiting to get j'ined.

' "These hosses of yours, sir, will be much improved by this!" says the clerk as he rode along, just a neck behind the pa'son. "'Twas a happy thought of your reverent mind to bring 'em out to-day. Why, it may be frosty and slippery in a day or two, and then the poor things mid not be able to leave the stable for weeks."

' "They may not, they may not, it is true. A merciful man is merciful to his beast," says the pa'son.

' "Hee, hee!" says the clerk, glancing sly into the pa'son's eye.

' "Ha, ha!" says the pa'son, a-glancing back into the clerk's. "Hal-loo!" he shouts, as he sees the fox break cover at that moment.

' "Halloo!" cries the clerk. "There he goes! Why, dammy, there's two foxes—"

' "Hush, clerk, hush! Don't let me hear that word again! Remember our calling."

' "True, sir, true. But really, good sport do carry away a man so, that he's apt to forget his high persuasion!" And the next minute the corner of the clerk's eye shot again into the corner of the pa'son's, and the pa'son's back again to the clerk's. "Hee, hee!" said the clerk.

' "Ha, ha!" said Pa'son Toogood.

' "Ah, sir," says the clerk again, "this is better than crying Amen to your Ever-and-ever on a winter's morning!"

' "Yes, indeed, clerk! To everything there's a season," says Pa'son Toogood, quite pat, for he was a learned Christian man when he liked, and had chapter and ve'se at his tongue's end, as a pa'son should.

'At last, late in the day, the hunting came to an end by the fox running into a' old woman's cottage, under her table, and up the clock-case. The pa'son and clerk were among the first in at the death, their faces a-staring in at the old woman's winder, and the clock striking as he'd never been heard to strik' before. Then came the question of finding their way home.

'Neither the pa'son nor the clerk knowed how they were going to do this, for their beasts were wellnigh tired down to the ground. But they started back-along as well as they could, though they were so done up that they could only drag along at a' amble, and not much of that at a time.

' "We shall never, never get there!" groaned Mr. Toogood, quite bowed down.

' "Never!" groans the clerk. "'Tis a judgment upon us for our iniquities!"

' "I fear it is," murmurs the pa'son.

'Well, 'twas quite dark afore they entered the pa'sonage gate, having crept into the parish as quiet as if they'd stole a hammer, little wishing their congregation to know what they'd been up to all day long. And as they were so dog-tired, and so anxious about the horses, never once did they think of the unmarried couple. As soon as ever the horses had been stabled and fed, and the pa'son and clerk had had a bit and a sup theirselves, they went to bed.

'Next morning when Pa'son Toogood was at breakfast, thinking of the glorious sport he'd had the day before, the clerk came in a hurry to the door and asked to see him.

' "It has just come into my mind, sir, that we've forgot all about the couple that we was to have married yesterday!"

'The half-chawed victuals dropped from the pa'son's mouth as if he'd been shot. "Bless my soul," says he, "so we have! How very awkward"!

' "It is, sir; very. Perhaps we've ruined the 'ooman!"

' "Ah – to be sure – I remember! She ought to have been married before."

' "If anything has happened to her up in that there tower, and no doctor or nuss —" '

('Ah – poor thing!' sighed the women.)

' "– 'twill be a quarter-sessions matter for us, not to speak of the disgrace to the Church!"

' "Good God, clerk, don't drive me wild!" says the pa'son. "Why the hell didn't I marry 'em, drunk or sober!" (Pa'sons used to cuss in them days like plain honest men.) "Have you been to the church to see what happened to them, or inquired in the village?"

' "Not I, sir! It only came into my head a moment ago, and I always like to be second to you in church matters. You could have knocked me down with a sparrow's feather when I thought o't, sir; I assure 'ee you could!"

'Well, the pa'son jumped up from his breakfast, and together they went off to the church.

' "It is not at all likely that they are there now," says Mr. Toogood, as they went; "and indeed I hope they are not. They be pretty sure to have escaped and gone home."

'However, they opened the church-hatch, entered the churchyard, and looking up at the tower there they seed a little small white face at the belfry-winder, and a little small hand waving. 'Twas the bride.

' "God my life, clerk," says Mr. Toogood. "I don't know how to face 'em!" And he sank down upon a tombstone. "How I wish I hadn't been so cussed particular!"

' "Yes – 'twas a pity we didn't finish it when we'd begun," the clerk said. "Still, since the feelings of your holy priestcraft wouldn't let ye, the couple must put up with it."

' "True, clerk, true! Does she look as if anything premature had took place?"

' "I can't see her no lower down than her arm-pits, sir."

' "Well – how do her face look?"

' "It do look mighty white!"

' "Well, we must know the worst! Dear me, how the small of my back do ache from that ride yesterday! . . . But to more godly business!"

'They went on into the church, and unlocked the tower stairs, and immediately poor Jane and Andrey busted out like starved mice from a cupboard, Andrey limp and sober enough now, and his bride pale and cold, but otherwise as usual.

' "What," says the pa'son with a great breath of relief, "you haven't been here ever since?"

' "Yes, we have, sir!" says the bride, sinking down upon a seat in her weakness. "Not a morsel, wet or dry, have we had since! It was impossible to get out without help, and here we've stayed!"

' "But why didn't you shout, good souls?" said the pa'son.

' "She wouldn't let me," says Andrey.

' "Because we were so ashamed at what had led to it," sobs Jane. "We felt that if it were noised abroad it would cling to us all our lives! Once or twice Andrey had a good mind to toll the bell, but then he said: 'No; I'll starve first. I won't bring disgrace on my name and yours, my dear.' And so we waited and waited, and walked round and round; but never did you come till now!"

' "To my regret!" says the pa'son. "Now, then, we will soon get it over."

' "I – I should like some victuals," said Andrey; "'twould gie me courage to do it, if it is only a crust o' bread and a' onion; for I am that leery that I can feel my stomach rubbing against my backbone."

' "I think we had better get it done," said the bride, a bit anxious in manner; "since we are all here convenient, too!"

'Andrey gave way about the victuals, and the clerk called in a second witness who wouldn't be likely to gossip about it, and soon the knot was tied, and the bride looked smiling and calm forthwith, and Andrey limper than ever.

' "Now," said Pa'son Toogood, "you two must come to my house, and have a good lining put to your insides before you go a step further."

'They were very glad of the offer, and went out of the churchyard by one path while the pa'son and clerk went out by the other, and so did not attract notice, it being still early. They entered the rectory as if they'd just come back from their trip to Port Bredy; and then they knocked in the victuals and drink till they could hold no more.

'It was a long while before the story of what they had gone through was known, but it was talked of in time, and they themselves laugh over it now; though what Jane got for her pains was no great bargain after all. 'Tis true she saved her name.'

'Was that the same Andrey who went to the squire's house as one of the Christmas fiddlers?' asked the seedsman.

'No, no,' replied Mr. Profitt, the schoolmaster. 'It was his father did that. Ay, it was all owing to his being such a man for eating and drinking.' Finding that he had the ear of the audience, the schoolmaster continued without delay: –

Old Andrey's Experience as a Musician

'I was one of the quire-boys at that time, and we and the players were to appear at the manor-house as usual that Christmas week, to play and sing in the hall to the Squire's people and visitors (among 'em being the archdeacon, Lord and Lady Baxby, and I don't know who); afterwards going, as we always did, to have a good supper in the servants' hall. Andrew knew this was the custom, and meeting us when we were starting to go, he said to us: "Lord, how I should like to join in that meal of beef, and turkey, and plum-pudding, and ale, that you happy ones be going to just now! One more or less will make no difference to the Squire. I am too old to pass as a singing boy, and too bearded to pass as a singing girl; can ye lend me a fiddle, neighbours, that I may come with ye as a bandsman?"

'Well, we didn't like to be hard upon him, and lent him an old one, though Andrew knew no more of music than the Giant o' Cernel; and armed with the instrument he walked up to the Squire's house with the others of us at the time appointed, and went in boldly, his fiddle under his arm. He made himself as natural as he could in opening the music-books and moving the candles to the best points for throwing light upon the notes; and all went well till we had played and sung "While shepherds watch", and "Star, arise", and "Hark the glad sound". Then the Squire's mother, a tall gruff old lady, who was much interested in church-music, said quite unexpectedly to Andrew: "My man, I see you don't play your instrument with the rest. How is that?"

'Every one of the quire was ready to sink into the earth with concern at the fix Andrew was in. We could see that he had fallen into a cold sweat, and how he would get out of it we did not know.

' "I've had a misfortune, mem," he says, bowing as meek as a child. "Coming along the road I fell down and broke my bow."

' "Oh, I am sorry to hear that," says she. "Can't it be mended?"

' "Oh no, mem," says Andrew. "'Twas broke all to splinters."

' "I'll see what I can do for you," says she.

'And then it seemed all over, and we played "Rejoice, ye drowsy mortals all", in D and two sharps. But no sooner had we got through it than she says to Andrew:

' "I've sent up into the attic, where we have some old musical instruments, and found a bow for you." And she hands the bow to poor wretched Andrew, who didn't even know which end to take hold of. "Now we shall have the full accompaniment," says she.

'Andrew's face looked as if it were made of rotten apple as he stood in the circle of players in front of his book; for if there was one person in the parish that everybody was afraid of, 'twas this hook-nosed old lady. However, by keeping a little behind the next man he managed to make pretence of beginning, sawing away with his bow without letting it touch the strings, so that it looked as if he were driving into the tune with heart and soul. 'Tis a question if he wouldn't have got through all right if one of the Squire's visitors (no other than the archdeacon) hadn't noticed that he held the fiddle upside down, the nut under his chin, and the tail-piece in his hand; and they began to crowd round him, thinking 'twas some new way of performing.

'This revealed everything; the Squire's mother had Andrew turned out of the house as a vile impostor, and there was great interruption to the harmony of the proceedings, the Squire declaring he should have notice to leave his cottage that day fortnight. However, when we got to the servants' hall there sat Andrew, who had been let in at the back door by the orders of the Squire's wife, after being turned out at the front by the orders of the Squire, and nothing more was heard about his leaving

Original settings of 19th century carols from the **Hardy Family and Puddletown Church Manuscripts: The Mellstock Carols.** *Hardy's father and grandfather had played in church bands at Stinsford and Puddletown; much of their music survives in their own manuscript copy.*

his cottage. But Andrew never performed in public as a musician after that night; and now he's dead and gone, poor man, as we all shall be!'

'I had quite forgotten the old choir, with their fiddles and bass-viols,' said the home-comer, musingly. 'Are they still going on the same as of old?'

'Bless the man!' said Christopher Twink, the master-thatcher; 'why, they've been done away with these twenty year. A young teetotaller plays the organ in church now, and plays it very well; though 'tis not quite such good music as in old times, because the organ is one of them that go with a winch, and the young teetotaller says he can't always throw the proper feeling into the tune without wellnigh working his arms off.'

'Why did they make the change, then?'

'Well, partly because of fashion, partly because the old musicians got into a sort of scrape. A terrible scrape 'twas, too – wasn't it, John? I shall never forget it – never! They lost their character as officers of the church as complete as if they'd never had any character at all.'

'That was very bad for them.'

'Yes.' The master-thatcher attentively regarded past times as if they lay about a mile off, and went on: –

Absent-mindedness in a Parish Choir

IT HAPPENED on Sunday after Christmas – the last Sunday ever they played in Longpuddle church gallery, as it turned out, though they didn't know it then. As you may know, sir, the players formed a very good band – almost as good as the Mellstock parish players that were led by the Dewys; and that's saying a great deal. There was Nicholas Puddingcome, the leader, with the first fiddle; there was Timothy Thomas, the bass-viol man; John Biles, the tenor fiddler, Dan'l Hornhead, with the serpent; Robert Dowdle, with the clarionet; and Mr. Nicks, with the oboe – all sound and powerful musicians, and strong-winded men – they that blowed. For that reason they were very much in demand Christmas week for little reels and dancing parties: for they could turn a jig or a hornpipe out of hand as well as ever they could turn out a psalm, and perhaps better, not to speak irreverent. In short, one half-hour they could be playing a Christmas carol in the Squire's hall to

A Few Crusted Characters

The gallery at Puddletown Church. Hardy would have known this church well. It is similar to the church in Absent-mindedness in a Parish Choir *with its musicians' gallery.*

the ladies and gentlemen, and drinking tay and coffee with 'em as modest as saints; and the next, at The Tinker's Arms, blazing away like wild horses with the "Dashing White Sergeant" to nine couple of dancers and more, and swallowing rum-and-cider hot as flame.

'Well, this Christmas they'd been out to one rattling randy after another every night, and had got next to no sleep at all. Then came the Sunday after Christmas, their fatal day. 'Twas so mortal cold that year that they could hardly sit in the gallery; for though the congregation down in the body of the church had a stove to keep off the frost, the players in the gallery had nothing at all. So Nicholas said at morning service, when 'twas freezing an inch an hour, "Please the Lord I won't stand this numbing weather no longer: this afternoon we'll have something in our insides to make us warm, if it cost a king's ransom."

'So he brought a gallon of hot brandy and beer, ready mixed, to church with him in the afternoon, and by keeping the jar well wrapped up in Timothy Thomas's bass-viol bag it kept drinkably warm till they wanted it, which was just a thimbleful in the Absolution, and another after the Creed, and the remainder at the beginning o' the sermon. When they'd had the last pull they felt quite comfortable and warm, and as the sermon went on – most unfortunately for 'em it was a long one that afternoon – they fell asleep, every man jack of 'em; and there they slept on as sound as rocks.

' 'Twas a very dark afternoon, and by the end of the sermon all you could see of the inside of the church were the pa'son's two candles alongside of him in the pulpit, and his spaking face behind 'em. The sermon being ended at last, the pa'son gie'd out the Evening Hymn. But no quire set about sounding up the tune, and the people began to turn their heads to learn the reason why, and then Levi Limpet, a boy who sat in the gallery, nudged Timothy and Nicholas, and said, "Begin! begin!"

' "Hey? what?" says Nicholas, starting up; and the church being so dark and his head so muddled he thought he was at the party they had played at all the night before, and away he went, bow and fiddle, at "The Devil among the Tailors", the favourite jig of our neighbourhood at that time. The rest of the band, being in the same state of mind and nothing doubting, followed their leader with all their strength, according to custom. They poured out that there tune till the lower bass notes of "The Devil among the Tailors" made the cobwebs in the roof shiver like ghosts; then Nicholas, seeing nobody moved, shouted out as he scraped (in his usual commanding way at dances when the folk didn't know the figures), "Top couples cross hands! And when I make the fiddle squeak at the end, every man kiss his pardner under the mistletoe!"

'The boy Levi was so frightened that he bolted down the gallery stairs and out homeward like lightning. The pa'son's hair fairly stood on end when he heard the evil tune raging through the church, and thinking the quire had gone crazy he held up his hand and said: "Stop, stop, stop! Stop, stop! What's this?" But they didn't hear'n for the noise of their own playing, and the more he called the louder they played.

'Then the folks came out of their pews, wondering down to the ground, and saying: "What do they mean by such wickedness! We shall be consumed like Sodom and Gomorrah!"

'And the Squire, too, came out of his pew lined wi' green baize, where lots of lords and ladies visiting at the house were worshipping along with him, and went and stood in front of the gallery, and shook his fist in the musicians' faces, saying, "What! In this reverent edifice! What!"

'And at last they heard'n through their playing, and stopped.

' "Never such an insulting, disgraceful thing – never!" says the Squire, who couldn't rule his passion.

' "Never!" says the pa'son, who had come down and stood beside him.

' "Not if the Angels of Heaven," says the Squire (he was a wickedish man, the Squire was, though now for once he happened to be on the Lord's side) – "not if the Angels of Heaven come down," he says, "shall one of you villainous players ever sound a note in this church again; for the insult to me, and my family, and my visitors, and the pa'son, and God Almighty, that you've a-perpetrated this afternoon!"

'Then the unfortunate church band came to their senses, and remembered where they were; and 'twas a sight to see Nicholas Puddingcome and Timothy Thomas and John Biles creep down the gallery stairs with their fiddles under their arms, and poor Dan'l Hornhead with his serpent, and Robert Dowdle with his clarionet, all looking as little as ninepins; and out they went. The pa'son might have forgi'ed 'em when he learned the truth o't, but the Squire would not. That very week he sent for a barrel-organ that would play two-and twenty new psalm-tunes, so exact and particular that, however sinful inclined you was, you could play nothing but psalm-tunes whatsoever. He had a really respectable man to turn the winch, as I said, and the old players played no more.'

'And, of course, my old acquaintance, the annuitant, Mrs. Winter, who always seemed to have something on her mind, is dead and gone?' said the home-comer, after a long silence.

Nobody in the van seemed to recollect the name.

'Oh yes, she must be dead long since: she was seventy when I as a child knew her,' he added.

'I can recollect Mrs. Winter very well, if nobody else can,' said the aged groceress. 'Yes, she's been dead these five-and-twenty year at least.

You knew what it was upon her mind, sir, that gave her that hollow-eyed look, I suppose?'

'It had something to do with a son of hers, I think I once was told. But I was too young to know particulars.'

The groceress sighed as she conjured up a vision of days long past. 'Yes,' she murmured, 'it had all to do with a son.' Finding that the van was still in a listening mood, she spoke on: –

The Winters and the Palmleys

To go back to the beginning – if one must – there were two women in the parish when I was a child, who were to a certain extent rivals in good looks. Never mind particulars, but in consequence of this they were at daggers-drawn, and they did not love each other any better when one of them tempted the other's lover away from her and married him. He was a young man of the name of Winter, and in due time they had a son.

'The other woman did not marry for many years: but when she was about thirty a quiet man named Palmley asked her to be his wife, and she accepted him. You don't mind when the Palmleys were Longpuddle folk, but I do well. She had a son also, who was, of course, nine or ten years younger than the son of the first. The child proved to be of rather weak intellect, though his mother loved him as the apple of her eye.

'This woman's husband died when the child was eight years old, and left his widow and boy in poverty. Her former rival, also a widow now, but fairly well provided for, offered for pity's sake to take the child as errand-boy, small as he was, her own son, Jack, being hard upon seventeen. Her poor neighbour could do no better than let the child go there. And to the richer woman's house little Palmley straightway went.

'Well, in some way or other – how, it was never exactly known – the thriving woman, Mrs. Winter, sent the little boy with a message to the next village one December day, much against his will. It was getting dark, and the child prayed to be allowed not to go, because he would be afraid coming home. But the mistress insisted, more out of thoughtlessness than cruelty, and the child went. On his way back he had to pass through Yalbury Wood, and something came out from behind a tree and frightened him into fits. The child was quite ruined by it; he became quite a drivelling idiot, and soon afterward died.

'Then the other woman had nothing left to live for, and vowed vengeance against that rival who had first won away her lover, and now had been the cause of her bereavement. This last affliction was certainly not intended by her thriving acquaintance, though it must be owned that when it was done she seemed but little concerned. Whatever vengeance poor Mrs. Palmley felt, she had no opportunity of carrying it out, and time might have softened her feelings into forgetfulness of her supposed wrongs as she dragged on her lonely life. So matters stood when, a year after the death of the child, Mrs. Palmley's niece, who had been born and bred in the city of Exonbury, came to live with her.

'This young woman – Miss Harriet Palmley – was a proud and handsome girl, very well brought up, and more stylish and genteel than the people of our village, as was natural, considering where she came from. She regarded herself as much above Mrs. Winter and her son in position as Mrs. Winter and her son considered themselves above poor Mrs. Palmley. But love is an unceremonious thing, and what in the world should happen but that young Jack Winter must fall woefully and wildly in love with Harriet Palmley almost as soon as he saw her.

'She, being better educated than he, and caring nothing for the village notion of his mother's superiority to her aunt, did not give him much encouragement. But Longpuddle being no very large world, the two could not help seeing a good deal of each other while she was staying there, and, disdainful young woman as she was, she did seem to take a little pleasure in his attentions and advances.

'One day when they were picking apples together, he asked her to marry him. She had not expected anything so practical as that at so early a time, and was led by her surprise into a half-promise; at any rate, she did not absolutely refuse him, and accepted some little presents that he made her.

'But he saw that her view of him was rather as a simple village lad than as a young man to look up to, and he felt that he must do something bold to secure her. So he said one day, "I am going away, to try to get into a better position than I can get here." In two or three weeks he wished her good-bye, and went away to Monksbury, to superintend a farm, with a view to start as a farmer himself; and from there he wrote regularly to her, as if their marriage were an understood thing.

'Now Harriet liked the young man's presents and the admiration of his eyes; but on paper he was less attractive to her. Her mother had been a schoolmistress, and Harriet had besides a natural aptitude for pen-and-ink work, in days when to be a ready writer was not such a common thing as it is now, and when actual handwriting was valued as an accomplishment in itself. Jack Winter's performances in the shape of love-letters quite jarred her city nerves and her finer taste, and when she answered one of them, in the lovely running hand that she took such pride in, she very strictly and loftily bade him to practise with a pen and spelling-book if he wished to please her. Whether he listened to her request or not nobody knows, but his letters did not improve. He ventured to tell her in his clumsy way that if her heart were more warm towards him she would not be so nice about his handwriting and spelling; which indeed was true enough.

'Well, in Jack's absence the weak flame that had been set alight in Harriet's heart soon sank low, and at last went out altogether. He wrote and wrote, and begged and prayed her to give a reason for her coldness; and then she told him plainly that she was town born, and he was not sufficiently well educated to please her.

'Jack Winter's want of pen-and-ink training did not make him less thin-skinned than others; in fact, he was terribly tender and touchy about anything. This reason that she gave for finally throwing him over grieved him, shamed him, and mortified him more than can be told in these times, the pride of that day in being able to write with beautiful flourishes, and the sorrow at not being able to do so, raging so high. Jack replied to her with an angry note, and then she hit back with smart little stings, telling him how many words he had misspelt in his last letter, and declaring again that this alone was sufficient justification for any woman to put an end to an understanding with him. Her husband must be a better scholar.

'He bore her rejection of him in silence, but his suffering was sharp – all the sharper in being untold. She communicated with Jack no more; and as his reason for going out into the world had been only to provide a home worthy of her, he had no further object in planning such a home now that she was lost to him. He therefore gave up the farming occupation by which he had hoped to make himself a master-farmer, and left the spot to return to his mother.

'As soon as he got back to Longpuddle he found that Harriet had already looked wi' favour upon another lover. He was a young road contractor, and Jack could not but admit that his rival was both in manners and scholarship much ahead of him. Indeed, a more sensible match for the beauty who had been dropped into the village by fate could hardly have been found than this man, who could offer her so much better a chance than Jack could have done, with his uncertain future and narrow abilities for grappling with the world. The fact was so clear to him that he could hardly blame her.

'One day by accident Jack saw on a scrap of paper the handwriting of Harriet's new beloved. It was flowing like a stream, well spelt, the work of a man accustomed to the ink-bottle and the dictionary, of a man already called in the parish a good scholar. And then it struck all of a sudden into Jack's mind what a contrast the letters of this young man must make to his own miserable old letters, and how ridiculous they must make his lines appear. He groaned and wished he had never written to her, and wondered if she had ever kept his poor performances. Possibly she had kept them, for women are in the habit of doing that, he thought, and whilst they were in her hands there was always a chance of his honest, stupid love-assurances to her being joked over by Harriet with her present lover, or by anybody who should accidentally uncover them.

'The nervous, moody young man could not bear the thought of it, and at length decided to ask her to return them, as was proper when engagements were broken off. He was some hours in framing, copying, and recopying the short note in which he made his request, and having finished it he sent it to her house. His messenger came back with the answer, by word of mouth, that Miss Palmley bade him say she should not part with what was hers, and wondered at his boldness in troubling her.

'Jack was much affronted at this, and determined to go for his letters himself. He chose a time when he knew she was at home, and knocked and went in without much ceremony; for though Harriet was so high and mighty, Jack had small respect for her aunt, Mrs. Palmley, whose little child had been his boot-cleaner in earlier days. Harriet was in the room, this being the first time they had met since she had jilted him. He asked for his letters with a stern and bitter look at her.

'At first she said he might have them for all that she cared, and took them out of the bureau where she kept them. Then she glanced over the outside one of the packet, and suddenly altering her mind, she told him shortly that his request was a silly one, and slipped the letters into her aunt's work-box, which stood open on the table, locking it and saying with a bantering laugh that of course she thought it best to keep 'em, since they might be useful to produce as evidence that she had good cause for declining to marry him.

'He blazed up hot. "Give me those letters!" he said. "They are mine!"

' "No, they are not," she replied: "they are mine."

' "Whos'ever they are I want them back," says he. "I don't want to be made sport of for my penmanship: you've another young man now! He has your confidence, and you pour all your tales into his ear. You'll be showing them to him!"

' "Perhaps," said my lady Harriet, with calm coolness, like the heartless woman that she was.

'Her manner so maddened him that he made a step towards the workbox, but she snatched it up, locked it in the bureau, and turned upon him triumphant. For a moment he seemed to be going to wrench the key of the bureau out of her hand; but he stopped himself, and swung round upon his heel and went away.

'When he was out-of-doors alone, and it got night, he walked about restless, and stinging with the sense of being beaten at all points by her. He could not help fancying her telling her new lover or her acquaintances of this scene with himself, and laughing with them over those poor blotted, crooked lines of his that he had been so anxious to obtain. As the evening passed on he worked himself into a dogged resolution to have them back at any price, come what might.

'At the dead of night he came out of his mother's house by the back door, and creeping through the garden hedge went along the field adjoining till he reached the back of her aunt's dwelling. The moon struck bright and flat upon the walls, 'twas said, and every shiny leaf of the creepers was like a little looking-glass in the rays. From long acquaintance Jack knew the arrangement and position of everything in Mrs. Palmley's house as well as in his own mother's. The back window close to him was a casement with little leaded squares, as it is to this day, and was, as now, one of two lighting the sitting-room. The other, being in front, was closed up with shutters, but this back one had not even a blind, and the moonlight as it streamed in showed every article of the furniture to him outside. To the right of the room is the fireplace, as you may remember; to the left was the bureau at that time; inside the bureau was Harriet's work-box, as he supposed (though it was really her aunt's), and inside the work-box were his letters. Well, he took out his pocket-knife, and without noise lifted the leading of one of the panes, so that he could take out the glass, and putting his hand through the hole he unfastened the casement, and climbed in through the opening. All the household – that is to say, Mrs. Palmley, Harriet, and the little maid-servant – were asleep. Jack went straight to the bureau, so he said, hoping it might have been unfastened again – it not being kept locked in ordinary – but Harriet had never unfastened it since she secured her letters there the day before. Jack told afterward how he thought of her asleep upstairs, caring nothing for him, and of the way she had made sport of him and of his letters; and having advanced so far, he was not to be hindered now. By forcing the large blade of his knife under the flap of the bureau, he burst the weak lock; within was the rosewood work-box just as she had placed it in her hurry to keep it from him. There being no time to spare for getting the letters out of it then, he took it under his arm, shut the bureau, and made the best of his way out of the house, latching the casement behind him, and refixing the pane of glass in its place.

'Winter found his way back to his mother's as he had come, and being dog-tired, crept upstairs to bed, hiding the box till he could destroy its contents. The next morning early he set about doing this, and carried it to the linhay at the back of his mother's dwelling. Here by the hearth he opened the box, and began burning one by one the letters that had cost him so much labour to write and shame to think of, meaning to return the box to Harriet, after repairing the slight damage he had caused it by opening it without a key, with a note – the last she would ever receive from him – telling her triumphantly that in refusing to return what he had asked for she had calculated too surely upon his submission to her whims.

'But on removing the last letter from the box he received a shock; for underneath it, at the very bottom, lay money – several golden guineas – "Doubtless Harriet's pocket-money," he said to himself; though it was not, but Mrs. Palmley's. Before he had got over his qualms at this discovery he heard footsteps coming through the house-passage to where he was. In haste he pushed the box and what was in it under some brushwood which lay in the linhay; but Jack had been already seen. Two constables entered the out-house, and seized him as he knelt before the fireplace, securing the work-box and all it contained at the same moment. They had come to apprehend him on a charge of breaking into the dwelling-house of Mrs. Palmley on the night preceding; and almost before the lad knew what had happened to him they were leading him along the lane that connects that end of the village with this turnpike road, and along they marched him between 'em all the way to Casterbridge jail.

'Jack's act amounted to night burglary – though he had never thought of it – and burglary was felony, and a capital offence in those days. His figure had been seen by some one against the bright wall as he came away from Mrs. Palmley's back window, and the box and money were found in his possession, while the evidence of the broken bureau-lock and tinkered window-pane was more than enough for circumstantial detail. Whether his protestation that he went only for his letters, which he believed to be wrongfully kept from him, would have availed him anything if supported by other evidence I do not know; but the one person who could have borne it out was Harriet, and she acted entirely under the sway of her aunt. That aunt was deadly towards Jack Winter. Mrs. Palmley's time had come. Here was her revenge upon the woman who had first won away her lover, and next ruined and deprived her of her heart's treasure – her little son. When the assize week drew on, and Jack had to stand his trial, Harriet did not appear in the case at all, which was allowed to take its course, Mrs. Palmley testifying to the general facts of the burglary. Whether Harriet would have come forward if Jack had appealed to her is not known; possibly she would have done it for pity's sake; but Jack was too proud to ask a single favour of a girl who had jilted him; and he let her alone. The trial was a short one, and the death sentence was passed.

'The day o' young Jack's execution was a cold dusty Saturday in March. He was so boyish and slim that they were obliged in mercy to hang him in the heaviest fetters kept in the jail, lest his heft should not break his neck, and they weighed so upon him that he could hardly drag himself up to the drop. At that time the gover'ment was not strict about burying the body of an executed person within the precincts of the prison, and at the earnest prayer of his poor mother his body was allowed to be brought home. All the parish waited at their cottage doors in the evening for its arrival: I remember how, as a very little girl, I stood by my mother's side. About eight o'clock, as we hearkened on our doorstones in the cold bright starlight, we could hear the faint crackle of a waggon from the direction of the turnpike-road. The noise was lost as the waggon dropped into a hollow, then it was plain again as it lumbered down the next long incline, and presently it entered Longpuddle. The coffin was laid in the belfry for the night, and the next day, Sunday, between the services, we buried him. A funeral sermon was preached the same afternoon, the text chosen being, "He was the only son of his mother, and she was a widow." . . . Yes, they were cruel times!

'As for Harriet, she and her lover were married in due time; but by all account her life was no jocund one. She and her good-man found that they could not live comfortably at Longpuddle, by reason of her connection with Jack's misfortunes, and they settled in a distant town, and were no more heard of by us; Mrs. Palmley, too, found it advisable to join 'em shortly after. The dark-eyed, gaunt old Mrs. Winter, remembered by the emigrant gentleman here, was, as you will have foreseen, the Mrs. Winter of this story; and I can well call to mind how lonely she was, how afraid the children were of her, and how she kept herself as a stranger among us, though she lived so long.'

'Longpuddle has had her sad experiences as well as her sunny ones,' said Mr. Lackland.

'Yes, yes. But I am thankful to say not many like that, though good and bad have lived among us.'

'There was Georgy Crookhill – he was one of the shady sort, as I have reason to know,' observed the registrar, with the manner of a man who would like to have his say also.

'I used to hear what he was as a boy at school.'

'Well, as he began so he went on. It never got so far as a hanging matter with him, to be sure; but he had some narrow escapes of penal servitude; and once it was a case of the biter bit.'

Incident in the life of Mr. George Crookhill

'ONE DAY,' the registrar continued, 'Georgy was ambling out of Melchester on a miserable screw,* the fair being just over, when he saw in front of him a fine-looking young farmer riding out of the town in the same direction. He was mounted on a good strong handsome animal, worth fifty guineas if worth a crown. When they were going up Bissett Hill, Georgy made it his business to overtake the young farmer. They passed the time o' day to one another; Georgy spoke of the state of the roads, and jogged alongside the well-mounted stranger in very friendly conversation. The farmer had not been inclined to say much to Georgy at first, but by degrees he grew quite affable, too – as friendly as Georgy was towards him. He told Crookhill that he had been doing business at Melchester fair, and was going on as far as Shottsford-Forum that night, so as to reach Casterbridge market the next day. When they came to Woodyates Inn they stopped to bait their horses, and agreed to drink together; with this they got more friendly than ever, and on they went again. Before they had nearly reached Shottsford it came on to rain, and as they were now passing through the village of Trantridge, and it was quite dark, Georgy persuaded the young farmer to go no further that night; the rain would most likely give them a chill. For his part he had heard that the little inn here was comfortable, and he meant to stay. At last the young farmer agreed to put up there also; and they dismounted, and entered, and had a good supper together, and talked over their affairs like men who had known and proved each other a long time. When it was the hour for retiring they went upstairs to a double-bedded room which Georgy Crookhill had asked the landlord to let them share, so sociable were they.

'Before they fell asleep they talked across the room about one thing and another, running from this to that till the conversation turned upon disguises, and changing clothes for particular ends. The farmer told Georgy that he had often heard tales of people doing it; but Crookhill professed to be very ignorant of all such tricks; and soon the young farmer sank into slumber.

'Early in the morning, while the tall young farmer was still asleep (I tell the story as 'twas told me), honest Georgy crept out of his bed by stealth, and dressed himself in the farmer's clothes, in the pockets of the

---

* screw: a broken-winded horse

said clothes being the farmer's money. Now though Georgy particularly wanted the farmer's nice clothes and nice horse, owing to a little transaction at the fair which made it desirable that he should not be too easily recognized, his desires had their bounds: he did not wish to take his young friend's money, at any rate more of it than was necessary for paying his bill. This he abstracted, and leaving the farmer's purse containing the rest on the bedroom table, went downstairs. The inn folks had not particularly noticed the faces of their customers, and the one or two who were up at this hour had no thought but that Georgy was the farmer; so when he had paid the bill very liberally, and said he must be off, no objection was made to his getting the farmer's horse saddled for himself; and he rode away upon it as if it were his own.

'About half an hour after, the young farmer awoke, and looking across the room saw that his friend Georgy had gone away in clothes which didn't belong to him, and had kindly left for himself the seedy ones worn by Georgy. At this he sat up in a deep thought for some time, instead of hastening to give an alarm. "The money, the money is gone," he said to himself, "and that's bad. But so are the clothes."

'He then looked upon the table and saw that the money, or most of it, had been left behind.

' "Ha, ha, ha!" he cried, and began to dance about the room. "Ha, ha, ha!" he said again, and made beautiful smiles to himself in the shaving-glass and in the brass candlestick; and then swung about his arms for all the world as if he were going through the sword exercise.

'When he had dressed himself in Georgy's clothes and gone downstairs, he did not seem to mind at all that they took him for the other; and even when he saw that he had been left a bad horse for a good one, he was not inclined to cry out. They told him his friend had paid the bill, at which he seemed much pleased, and without waiting for breakfast he mounted Georgy's horse and rode away likewise, choosing the nearest by-lane in preference to the highroad, without knowing that Georgy had chosen that by-lane also.

'He had not trotted more than two miles in the personal character of Georgy Crookhill when, suddenly rounding a bend that the lane made thereabout, he came upon a man struggling in the hands of two village constables. It was his friend Georgy, the borrower of his clothes and horse. But so far was the young farmer from showing any alacrity in rushing forward to claim his property that he would have turned the poor beast he rode into the wood adjoining, if he had not been already perceived. ' "Help, help, help!" cried the constables. "Assistance in the name of the Crown!"

'The young farmer could do nothing but ride forward. "What's the matter?" he inquired, as coolly as he could.

' "A deserter – a deserter!" said they. "One who's to be tried by court-martial and shot without parley. He deserted from the Dragoons at Cheltenham some days ago, and was tracked; but the search-party can't find him anywhere, and we told 'em if we met him we'd hand him on to 'em forthwith. The day after he left the barracks the rascal met a respectable farmer and made him drunk at an inn, and told him what a fine soldier he would make, and coaxed him to change clothes, to see how well a military uniform would become him. This the simple farmer did; when our deserter said that for a joke he would leave the room and go to the landlady, to see if she would know him in that dress. He never came back, and Farmer Jollice found himself in soldier's clothes, the money in his pockets gone, and, when he got to the stable, his horse gone, too."

' "A scoundrel!" says the young man in Georgy's clothes. "And is this the wretched caitiff?" (pointing to Georgy).

' "No, no!" cries Georgy, as innocent as a babe of this matter of the soldier's desertion. "He's the man! He was wearing Farmer Jollice's suit o' clothes, and he slept in the same room wi' me, and brought up the subject of changing clothes, which put it into my head to dress myself in his suit before he was awake. He's got on mine!"

' "D'ye hear the villain?" groans the tall young man to the constables. "Trying to get out of his crime by charging the first innocent man with it that he sees! No, master soldier – that won't do!"

' "No, no! That won't do!" the constables chimed in. "To have the impudence to say such as that, when we caught him in the act almost! But, thank God, we've got the handcuffs on him at last."

' "We have, thank God," said the tall young man. "Well, I must move on. Good luck to ye with your prisoner!" And off he went, as fast as his poor jade would carry him.

'The constables then, with Georgy handcuffed between 'em, and leading the horse, marched off in the other direction, towards the village where they had been accosted by the escort of soldiers sent to bring the deserter back, Georgy groaning: "I shall be shot, I shall be shot!" They had not gone more than a mile before they met them.

' "Hoi, there!" says the head constable.

' "Hoi, yerself!" says the corporal in charge.

' "We've got your man," says the constable.

' "Where?" says the corporal.

' "Here, between us," said the constable. "Only you don't recognize him out o' uniform."

'The corporal looked at Georgy hard enough; then shook his head and said he was not the absconder.

' "But the absconder changed clothes with Farmer Jollice, and took his horse; and this man has 'em, d'ye see!"

' "'Tis not our man," said the soldiers. "He's a tall young fellow with a mole on his right cheek, and a military bearing, which this man decidedly has not."

' "I told the two officers of justice that 'twas the other!" pleaded Georgy. "But they wouldn't believe me."

'And so it became clear that the missing dragoon was the tall young farmer, and not Georgy Crookhill – a fact which Farmer Jollice himself corroborated when he arrived on the scene. As Georgy had only robbed the robber, his sentence was comparatively light. The deserter from the Dragoons was never traced: his double shift of clothing having been of the greatest advantage to him in getting off; though he left Georgy's horse behind him a few miles ahead, having found the poor creature more hindrance than aid.'

There was now a lull in the discourse, and soon the van descended the hill leading into the long straggling village. When the houses were reached the passengers dropped off one by one, each at his or her own door. Arrived at the inn, the returned emigrant secured a bed, and having eaten a light meal, sallied forth upon the scene he had known so well in his early days. Though flooded with the light of the rising moon, none of the objects wore the attractiveness in this their real presentation that had ever accompanied their images in the field of his imagination when he was more than two thousand miles removed from them. The peculiar charm attaching to an old village in an old country, as seen by the eyes of an absolute foreigner, was lowered in his case by magnified expectations from infantine memories. He walked on, looking at this chimney and that old wall, till he came to the churchyard, which he entered.

The head-stones, whitened by the moon, were easily decipherable; and now for the first time Lackland began to feel himself amid the village community that he had left behind him five-and-thirty years before. Here, beside the Sallets, the Darths, the Pawles, the Privetts, the Sargents, and others of whom he had just heard, were names he remembered even better than those: the Jickses, and the Crosses, and the Knights, and the Olds. Doubtless representatives of these families, or some of them, were yet among the living; but to him they would all be as strangers. Far from finding his heart ready-supplied with roots and tendrils here, he perceived that in returning to this spot it would be incumbent upon him to re-establish himself from the beginning, precisely as though he had never known the place, nor it him. Time had not condescended to wait his pleasure, nor local life his greeting.

The figure of Mr. Lackland was seen at the inn, and in the village street, and in the fields and lanes about Upper Longpuddle, for a few days after his arrival, and then, ghost-like, it silently disappeared. He had told some of the villagers that his immediate purpose in coming had been fulfilled by a sight of the place, and by conversation with its inhabitants; but that his ulterior purpose – of coming to spend his latter days among them – would probably never be carried out. It is now a dozen or fifteen years since his visit was paid, and his face has not again been seen.

March 1891

RINGWOOD SCHOOL
GRANT MAINTAINED COMPREHENSIVE
LIBRARY